IRISH
Cooking

BIDDY WHITE LENNON

BONECHI

O'BRIEN

Distributed by
The O'Brien Press Ltd., 12 Terenure Road East,
Rathgar, Dublin 6, Ireland
Tel. +353 1 4923333; Fax +353 1 4922777;
e-mail: books@obrien.ie; Website: www.obrien.ie
ISBN 978-1-84717-024-8

© Copyright by Casa Editrice Bonechi
Via dei Cairoli, 18/b – Firenze – Italia
Tel. +39 055576841 – Fax +39 0555000766
e-mail: bonechi@bonechi.it
Internet: www.bonechi.com
ISBN 978-88-476-2042-1

Publication created by Casa Editrice Bonechi
Publication Manager: Monica Bonechi
Photographic Research: Editorial Staff
of Casa Editrice Bonechi
Graphic design, layout and cover:
Andrea Agnorelli
Editing: Elena Rossi, Mary Webb
Text by Biddy White Lennon

Dietician: Dr. John Luke Hili
In the kitchen: Lisa Mugnai

Printed in Italy by Centro Stampa Editoriale
Bonechi.

PHOTOGRAPHY ACKNOWLEDGEMENTS
Photographs from archives of Casa Editrice
Bonechi taken by *Monica Bonechi, Andrea
Fantauzzo* and *Ghigo Roli.*
Credits:
Avoca Shop, Suffolk Street, Dublin: pages 2
centre bottom, 29 bottom right.
Photos courtesy of:
Guinness Storehouse: pages 94 bottom, 95 centre
right; *O'Brien Press Ltd.:* pages 67 and 88.

The publisher apologises for any omissions
and is willing to make amends with the
formal recognition of the author of any photo
subsequently identified.

KEY TO SYMBOLS:

DIFFICULTY	FLAVOUR	NUTRITIONAL VALUE
● EASY	● MILD	● LOW
●● MEDIUM	●● MEDIUM	●● MEDIUM
●●● DIFFICULT	●●● STRONG	●●● HIGH

Preparation and cooking times are shown in hours (hr) and minutes
(e. g. 30' is 30 minutes). Proteins and fats are shown in grammes.

IRELAND
THE FOOD ISLAND

"Let the food be fresh and the drink be
aged" (An old Irish saying)

*Ireland is a small island on the sea-
board of Europe. But "Ireland – the
food island" is more than a clever mar-
keting slogan – it characterises an ancient Irish attitude to food. The superb
quality of the food that grows naturally
in the country means that
the Irish have always preferred food simply prepared
and served. Ireland has always been a food-exporting
nation. Today its
grass-fed beef
and lamb, its
dairy produce,
its farmhouse
cheeses and arti-
san smoked and
cured foods are
exported all over
the world and the
fresh fish caught
in the clean Atlantic waters round the
coast are coveted by other nations.*

*Irish animals graze on grass and herb-
age for most of the year, living naturally
in our fields, hillsides and mountain-
sides; this is what makes Irish meat so
good to eat. Meat has been central to
Irish food culture for thousands of years.
The Celts, however, valued cattle above
all other animals.
A pastoral farm-
ing system emerged
and brought a great
emphasis on bán-
bhianna ('white
meats' made from
milk). The Nor-
mans brought more
advanced agricultur-
al methods, placed
great emphasis on sheep and introduced
new breeds of domesticated and game
animals and birds. Agricultural practice
changed again and for a century or so
most of the land reared huge herds of
cattle and sheep for export. The native Irish, by
now existing
on tiny small-
holdings, de-
pended on pork
and bacon from
the family pig
to provide what
small quantities
of meat they ate.
Their ingenuity in cur-
ing (salting) and spic-
ing pig meat and fish
outstripped their use of
sheep meat, beef, wild
game and fowl.*

*Colonisation by the English in Tudor
times and the following centuries meant
that two food cultures emerged. The
'Big houses' of the Anglo-Irish land-
lords were well supplied with meat,
farmyard fowl and game and had
cold-store rooms, elaborate facilities
for cooking and the money to employ
trained cooks and servants. For the
overwhelming majority living in cabins
and cottages, whose cooking facilities
were a turf-fuelled open fire and a hearth
wide enough for smoking meat, meals
were very simple and limited to what
they could rear or gather. The introduc-
tion of the potato began the destruction
of the food culture based on beef and
milk, of the Gaelic-speaking native Irish
but simple one-pot dishes flavoured with
wild herbs, fruit and nuts survived. So,*

too, did the traditional craft of curing and smoking and (for those who could afford it) spicing meat.

The Irish have always been willing to take from foreign influences; what the Irish ate, at any time, was determined by the way they were living. It was probably fish and shellfish that brought the first settlers to Ireland; it was the people's semi nomadic, pastoral way of life that made bánbhianna (white meats made from milk) predominate in their diet in our heroic age. The grains, the wild and the cultivated fruits and vegetables from the early Christian monastery tradition, and the game animals, birds and fish brought in by the Normans are also still prominent in Irish cooking. When the potato came along, we ate it almost to the exclusion of other foods. It was the catastrophe of the potato famines that finally destroyed what was left of the ancient way of life and the period immediately afterwards was when our older food traditions were finally lost. With the return of relative prosperity in the middle of the 20th century, we relegated the potato to an accompaniment to other foods, but we had access to a limited amount of traditional recipes to fall back upon.

Bread is at the root of the Irish baking tradition, but the range of scones, tarts, cakes and biscuits baked in the home remains astonishing. It is true that traditional Irish baking is on the plain side; the ability of a home baker to produce a good loaf of brown bread is far more highly prized than fancy cakes. The confections developed in other European food cultures are not for the Irish. Yet, when you consider the fairly limited range of ingredients used – wheat and oat flour, eggs, potatoes, honey, the fresh fruits, berries and nuts that thrive in our climate (like apples, pears, rhubarb, raspberries, strawberries, fraughans (blueberries) and (given shelter) figs, hazelnuts and walnuts) – the subtle variations in flavour and texture make it a baking tradition to be proud of.

Historically there is no such thing as a 'definitive' recipe for any traditional Irish dish. Some of the recipes of some very individual Irish cooks who were employed in one or other 'Big House' have survived. These tell us how they prepared some dishes but most often are a simple record of the ingredients used. What is constant, however, are their methods of preparation.

After the heroic age with its freshly dug seething pits (fulucht fiadb) which were filled with water and brought up to seething point with fire-heated stones, the traditional Irish home had very limited means of cooking: an open turf fire, a large iron pot (a bastible) which could be suspended at different heights above the fire or its embers, a flat iron griddle which could be similarly adjusted, and sometimes a chimney, but more usually just the rafters, for smoking meat and fish. The (relatively) big house of a prosperous farmer might have a spit for roasting meats in front of an open fire and some kind of crude, directly heated oven, usually off the chimney.

Cooking techniques were, inevitably, simple: griddle breads or 'cakes'; ways of extending the life of seasonal food-

Top, the Spire in O'Connell Street. Top left, a traditional Irish pub in Wexford.
Opposite page, some shamrock, an Irish emblem, traditionally worn on St Patrick's Day. Two baskets of bread from the Avoca shop, Suffolk Street, Dublin.

stuffs by smoking, salting and curing; and dishes for 'keeping', or for quick and simple meals. Most recipes were 'one-pot' in the style of peasant cooking everywhere (for which the potato was supremely suited) and based on ingredients in season.

Ireland is a relatively small country and there are no 'regions' (terroirs) when it comes to traditional foods. With a few exceptions most of the dishes in this book are eaten in all parts of the country, with no more than slight variations in ingredients, accompaniments and seasonings. The recipes in this book are dishes that are regularly cooked and eaten in Irish homes: traditional fish and meat dishes, potato dishes, breads and baking, puddings and desserts, as well as more elaborate dishes once cooked only in the 'Big House' which are now cooked in many Irish homes for special occasions.

TABLE OF CONTENTS

Breakfasts

Adare, County Limerick.

Nowadays the Irish breakfast can be anything from a bowl of porridge oats or a hurried slice of buttered toast and a cup of tea in the family home before the daily commute to work, to a gourmet feast in a five-star hotel or guesthouse. While 'The Full Irish' breakfast of bacon, sausages, eggs etc would once have been the standard daily breakfast of many people, most nowadays would eat this only as a weekend treat or as 'brunch' (a combination of breakfast and lunch).

Porridge

■ 40 g/1 ½ oz/½ cup oatflakes
■ 375 ml/1 ½ cups cold water or milk
■ a pinch of salt

Serves: 1
Preparation: ½'
Cooking: 3 ½' or 6'
Difficulty: ●
Flavour: ●
Kcal (per serving): 389
Proteins (per serving): 18
Fats (per serving): 14
Nutritional Value: ●●

*P*lace oatflakes and liquid in a saucepan and stir. Bring to boiling point, then simmer for about 6 minutes, stirring regularly. Add salt near the end. Serve hot with cream and honey or with a compote of stewed fruit like apples, rhubarb, or berries.

MICROWAVE METHOD:

Place oatflakes and liquid in a largish bowl and stir. Cook at 600 watts for 3 ½ minutes or at 800 watts for 2 ½ minutes. Stir halfway through cooking time. Stand for 2 minutes before serving. Note: If cooking double the amount, it will take double the time.

Pinhead Oatmeal Porridge

Serves: 4
Preparation: ½'
Cooking: 30'
Difficulty: ●
Flavour: ●
Kcal (per serving): 159
Proteins (per serving): 5
Fats (per serving): 3
Nutritional Value: ●

- 135 g/4 ¾ oz/1 cup pinhead oatmeal
- 1 ltr/4 cups water
- 1 level teasp salt

*B*ring the water to the boil in a pot. Slowly sprinkle in the oatmeal, stirring rapidly all the time to prevent lumps. Simmer for 30 minutes, adding salt near the end. Cook until it has reached the consistency that you like. Serve hot with cream, honey, brown sugar or stewed fruit.

Long before the arrival of the potato, oats were the Irish winter staple and were used in lots of ways. Whole oats were ground, the chaff discarded, leaving the "groats". When these are chopped into pieces they are called pinhead, or coarse, oatmeal. These may then be ground into oat flour, or steamed and rolled into oatflakes. Porridge is made with either pinhead oatmeal or with oatflakes, which, because they cook faster, are more commonly used for making porridge today. Porridge is a simple, nutritious dish, and thanks to the new status of oats as a health food, it's as popular today as it ever was – a warming and sustaining breakfast.

On market day the local farmers still gather to exchange gossip and strike bargains.

The Full Irish Breakfast

Serves: 4

Preparation: 1'

Cooking 10'

Difficulty: ●

Flavour: ●●

Kcal (per serving): 1256

Proteins (per serving): 45

Fats (per serving): 85

Nutritional Value: ●●●

- 4 rashers of back bacon, (preferably dry cured, with the rinds snipped with a scissors every 2 cm/1 inch to stop them curling)
- 4 rashers of streaky bacon (preferably dry cured and snipped as above)
- 8 pork breakfast sausages
- 4 tomatoes, halved
- 4 slices of black pudding, 2 cm/1 inch thick
- 4 slices of white pudding, 2 cm/1 inch thick
- 4 eggs, fried or poached
- 4 small slices of bread
- 4 small potato cakes (optional) (see recipe page 12)
- a little butter or oil

Grill the tomatoes, sausages and puddings. Start the tomatoes cut-side down and halfway through cooking turn the cut side up. Sausages and puddings are turned carefully so that they brown evenly on all sides. In a frying pan heat a little bacon fat (or butter, or olive oil). Fry the bread or potato cakes in this until crisp and brown. Lay the rashers on top of the cooked sausages and puddings and grill until the fat is crisp and the meat cooked. Meanwhile add a little more fat to the pan and fry the eggs on one side only, basting occasionally with the fat; these are cooked to taste, but most Irish people like them with the yolk still soft. Serve the rashers, sausages, tomatoes and puddings with the fried eggs (on top of the fried bread) and accompanied with plenty of wholemeal brown bread and butter and a large pot of strong tea.

The Ulster Fry

- 4 rashers of back bacon, (preferably dry cured, with the rinds snipped with a scissors every 2 cm/1 inch to stop them curling)
- 4 rashers of streaky bacon (preferably dry cured and snipped as above)
- 8 pork breakfast sausages
- 4 tomatoes, halved
- 4 slices of black pudding, 2 cm/1 inch thick
- 4 slices of white pudding, 2 cm/1 inch thick
- 4 eggs, fried or poached
- a little butter or oil
- 110 g/4 oz mushrooms (preferably large, mature, open-capped mushrooms)
- 4 potato cakes, or small boxty breads (see recipes pages 12 and 19)
- 2 farls of griddle bread/soda farls (see recipe page 29)

If you thought 'The Full Irish' a very large breakfast it's only in the halfpenny place in comparison to the breakfast that would be eaten in Ulster!

Cook the sausages, rashers, puddings, tomatoes and eggs in the same way as for the Full Irish breakfast.

1 Slice the mushrooms (or leave whole, but they'll take much longer to cook) and pan-fry them in very little butter. The mushrooms will absorb the butter and begin to brown, so don't be tempted to add more butter. In another pan, fry the potato cakes in butter or bacon fat.

2 Split the farls of griddle bread horizontally and fry them in bacon fat too.

Serves: 4
Preparation: 5'
Cooking: 15'
Difficulty: ●
Flavour: ●●
Kcal (per serving): 1601
Proteins (per serving): 53
Fats (per serving): 101
Nutritional Value: ●●●

Kippers

Serves: 4
Preparation: ½'
Cooking: 3'
Difficulty: ●
Flavour: ●●
Kcal (per serving): 363
Proteins (per serving): 27
Fats (per serving): 27
Nutritional Value: ●●●

- 4 large, or 8 small, kipper fillets, undyed
- 4 teasp unsalted butter
- black pepper, to taste
- butter, to taste (preferably farmhouse butter)

*K*ippers are eaten warm and may be grilled, pan-fried, or heated the traditional way in just-boiled water.

1 Choose a tall, heatproof jug large enough to hold the kipper fillets vertically. Warm the jug, place kippers in the jug and then pour in boiling water so that it comes up to the top of the kipper fillets. Leave to stand for about 3 minutes (no more).

2 Lift from the water and pat dry with kitchen paper. Place on hot plates with a little pat of butter on top of each fillet (chopped fresh parsley and dill leaves too, if you have them). Accompany with wholemeal soda bread and butter.

To grill kippers, brush a little melted butter on top of each fillet and heat under a medium grill for 2-3 minutes until hot through but not browned.
To pan fry, heat a frying pan large enough to hold all the fillets and melt the butter in it. Place the kippers, skin side down, in the warmed butter and heat over a medium heat for 2-3 minutes, or until hot through but not browned.

Smoked Salmon

Serves: 4
Preparation: ½'
Difficulty: ●
Flavour: ●●
Kcal (per serving): 399
Proteins (per serving): 30
Fats (per serving): 15
Nutritional Value: ●●●

- 450 g/1 lb smoked salmon
- 1 large lemon
- freshly ground black pepper
- wholemeal soda bread and butter

*I*f the salmon is not pre-sliced, slice it very, very thinly and lay on plates. Serve with buttered slices of brown soda bread, lemon wedges, and a pepper mill; allow everyone to grind black pepper over the salmon to their taste. Many people use paprika instead of pepper but this would not be traditional or recommended.

Salmon farming in Glenarm, County Antrim.

Smoked Salmon with Potato Cakes

- 8 slices of smoked salmon
- 8 small potato cakes, served hot
- 125 ml/4 fl oz/½ cup sour cream, or crème fraîche
- 2 tablesp chives, finely chopped
- freshly ground black pepper

for the potato cakes:
- 450 g/1 lb floury potatoes, cooked, and mashed hot
- 60-175 g/2-6 oz/½-1 ½ cups plain white flour
- ¾ teasp salt, or to taste
- 2 tablesp butter, melted
- 60 ml/2 fl oz/¼ cup milk (approximately)

1 To make the potato cakes, reserve two tablespoons of the flour and mix all the other ingredients together, adding just enough milk to make a fairly firm dough. Sprinkle the reserved flour on a flat surface and roll out the dough on it until it is 0.5-1 cm/¼-½ inch thick. Cut into square, triangular, or round shapes as you wish. Bake on an ungreased griddle (or heavy frying pan) until lightly brown on both sides. Serve hot from the pan, or reheat by frying on a pan in a little bacon fat or butter.

They may also be reheated in the oven or under a grill (spread with very little butter and cooked until just hot through). This amount will make 8-12, depending on the thickness and shape chosen.

2 To assemble the dish, mix the sour cream (or crème fraîche) and chives and season with black pepper. Place a slice of smoked salmon on each potato cake, folding over if necessary so that it fits neatly on top. Spoon the sour cream (or crème fraîche) mixture on top.

This dish can also be served as a starter or a light snack.

Serves: 4
Preparation: 15′
Cooking: 10′
Difficulty: ●
Flavour: ●●
Kcal (per serving): 448
Proteins (per serving): 17
Fats (per serving): 18
Nutritional Value: ●●●

Buttermilk and Oatmeal Pancakes

- 600 ml/20 fl oz/2 ¼ cups buttermilk (or sour milk)
- 150 g/5 oz/1 cup finely ground oatmeal
- 100 g/3 ½ oz /generous ¾ cup self-raising flour
- 2-3 tablesp honey
- 1 teasp bicarbonate of soda
- 1 medium egg, beaten
- enough milk to turn the mixture to a fairly thin batter

Makes: 10-15 (depending on size)

Preparation: 5' (plus overnight soaking time for the oatmeal)

Cooking: 2' for each batch of pancakes

Difficulty: ●

Flavour: ●

Kcal: 184

Proteins: 8

Fats: 5

Nutritional Value: ●●●

*P*lace buttermilk in a bowl, then add the oatmeal; mix well and leave to soak overnight.

1 The next day, sift together the flour and the baking soda and mix them into the oatmeal batter.

2 Add the honey, the beaten egg and just enough milk to make a batter that is slightly thinner than for ordinary pancakes or crepes. Lightly grease a heavy pan or griddle with butter; heat over a medium heat and when it is hot place tablespoonfuls of the batter on it. Leave them until they rise and are covered in bubbles and little holes on top. Turn over to brown on the other side. Best eaten hot from the pan with butter and honey, or with honey and whipped cream or accompanied by a fruit compote.

Note: if ground oatmeal is not available, simply grind pinhead oatmeal in a food processor.

Pancakes

- 2 medium eggs, beaten
- 110 g/4 oz/scant 1 cup plain flour
- 125 ml/4 fl oz/½ cup milk
- 125 ml/4 fl oz/½ cup water
- 15 ml/1 tablesp melted butter

Put the flour into a bowl, make a well in the centre and pour in the beaten eggs. Whisk the eggs and flour until you have a thick paste. Mix the milk and water and slowly whisk into the egg and flour paste. You should end up with a batter that has the consistency of thin (single) cream. Allow to stand for a little while.

Makes: 10-12

Preparation: 3'

Cooking: 1-2' for each pancake

Difficulty: ●

Flavour: ●

Kcal: 89

Proteins: 4

Fats: 4

Nutritional Value: ●●●

Heat a frying pan until it is quite hot. Wipe the pan with folded kitchen paper dipped in melted butter so that it is evenly greased. Pour about two tablespoons of the batter onto the hot pan, then tilt it rapidly so that the batter spreads evenly over the base. Cook over a medium heat until the pancake surface has bubbles and little holes all over. Turn with a palette knife and cook the other side for slightly less time. Serve and eat each pancake while it is hot, sprinkled with sugar and lemon juice.

Cooked pancakes will keep for two or three days in the fridge and can be reheated. Pancakes are a popular dish, and when served with a savoury or a sweet filling are also eaten as a light meal or a dessert.

SUGGESTIONS FOR FILLINGS:

Spread 1-2 tablespoons of cooked puréed apple, stewed rhubarb, or a berry compote along the centre of each pancake, then roll it up. Pour a few tablespoons of apple juice into a well-buttered rectangular baking dish. Arrange the pancake rolls in one layer in the dish and reheat in an oven set to 180°C/350°F/Gas 4 until hot through.

A savoury filling for pancakes, such as a creamy fish pie filling, should be reheated in a little cream instead of apple juice.

Potatoes

Some fine thoroughbreds at the National Stud, Kildare.

Potatoes are now central to Irish food culture yet their use is of relatively recent origin. Before potatoes were introduced to Ireland in the 17th century, the Irish ate far more grains: oats, wheat, rye and barley. But, just as Italians are devoted to pasta, the Irish are now devoted to potatoes and are particularly fond of "floury" potatoes. These are varieties with a low moisture, high dry-matter content. Most of the traditional recipes can be made successfully only with floury potatoes rather than the moist, "waxy" potatoes favoured in other food cultures.

At the start of the potato harvest, in early summer, "new" potatoes with a higher moisture content do come to market. These are prized for their flavour and eaten simply boiled, or steamed. Main crop potatoes mature later and are usually called "old" potatoes.

In Ireland potatoes are boiled "in their skins" ie, unpeeled. After cooking, the potatoes are usually peeled at the table and the skins left on a side plate (a method that preserves the nutritional value of the potato). In old days people who lived by the sea boiled their potatoes in sea water because it is said that this prevented the skin from splitting or cracking, so none of the mineral content is lost. People who are used to cooking firm, waxy (usually yellow-fleshed) potatoes may find cooking floury ones a challenge as they have a tendency to collapse.

Boiled or Steamed Potatoes

To boil "old" (main crop) potatoes:

■ 4 very large, 8 medium, or 12 small potatoes
■ salt

*C*lean and wash thoroughly but do not peel. Discard any with black or green discoloration and remove any sprouts. Cover with cold water. Add enough salt to make the water quite salty. Cover the pot and bring to the boil; boil steadily until tender. Drain at once and dry by placing a clean tea-towel on top and leaving them on a very low heat for a few minutes. Do not replace the lid. Boiled potatoes must be served as soon as cooked. If the recipe requires them to be mashed or peeled always do this while the potatoes are hot.

Serves: 4
Preparation: 2′
Cooking time: 20′-30′
*   or until tender (depends on size)*
Difficulty: ●
Flavour: ●
Kcal (per serving): 382
Proteins (per serving): 11
Fats (per serving): 1
Nutritional Value: ●●

To boil "new" potatoes:

*C*lean and wash the potatoes. Do not peel them. Have ready a pot of boiling, salted water, just enough to cover the potatoes. Put potatoes into the boiling water and bring back to the boil quickly; boil steadily until tender. Drain, then place a tea-towel on top of the potatoes and leave them to dry over a very low heat for just a few minutes.

Steamed Potatoes

In Ireland potatoes are never served al dente but cooked until fully tender. As the interval between the skin splitting and the potato collapsing into a mush is short, the answer is to steam them. Steaming takes a little longer, but it's a small price to pay to achieve what is called a "laughing potato", where the skin splits a little but the potato keeps its shape.

Place boiling water in the bottom of the pot and the washed potatoes in the steamer; steam until tender. Dry in the usual manner. Steamed potatoes will keep for longer without spoiling. Simply pull the steamer off the heat but do not drain or dry them until you are ready to serve.

Traditionally, potatoes cooked in their skins (boiled or steamed) are served with a small side plate placed on the left-hand side of the dinner plate. The potatoes are taken from a potato ring or serving dish onto this plate and peeled using a knife and fork. The skins are left on the side plate and the potato is lifted onto the dinner plate.

Greencastle, a 13th century ruined fortress that guards the north side of Carlingford Lough, County Down.

Little Potato Pancakes

*W*hisk together the eggs, flour, baking powder and about half the milk. Quickly stir in the mashed potatoes and mix really well. Add enough milk to make a thick batter. Season with salt and freshly ground black pepper. Choose a wide non-stick pan or griddle; heat it and grease lightly. Drop as many tablespoonfuls of the batter as you can fit onto the hot griddle. Cook for about 3 minutes or until bubbles rise to the surface and the underside is well browned. Turn over with a palette knife and brown the other side. Keep hot while you cook the rest of the batter.

- 4 large floury potatoes, cooked and mashed while hot
- 2 eggs
- 3 ½ tablesp plain white flour
- 1 teasp baking powder
- 200 ml/7 fl oz/¾ cup of milk
- salt and freshly ground black pepper

ADDITIONAL FLAVOURINGS:
Add chopped scallions (spring onions), crisply-cooked and finely chopped bacon rashers, or cooked (and finely chopped) mushrooms.

Serves: 4 (makes 20)

Preparation: 3'

Cooking: 5-10'

Difficulty: ●

Flavour: ●

Kcal (per serving): 390

Proteins (per serving): 15

Fats (per serving): 7

Nutritional Value: ●●

Boxty

Makes: 8 farls
Preparation: 20' (plus 1-2 hours
    waiting time for starch to settle)
Cooking: 30'-40'
Difficulty: ●●
Flavour: ●
Kcal (per serving): 347
Proteins (per serving): 9
Fats (per serving): 6
Nutritional Value: ●●

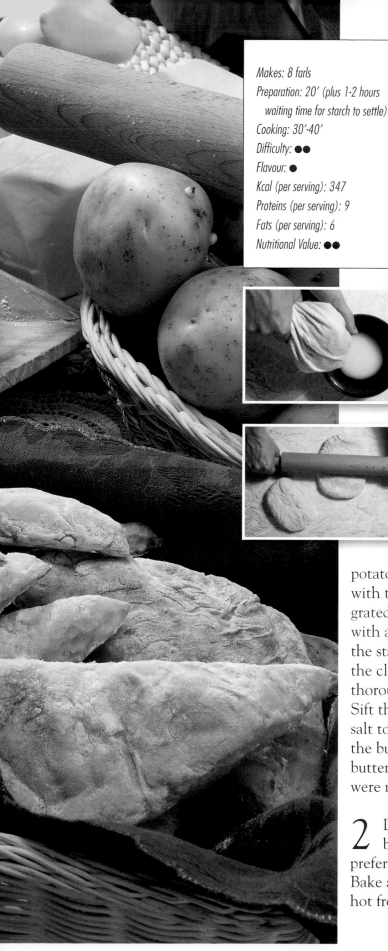

- 225 g/8 oz floury potatoes, grated raw
- 225 g/8 oz floury potatoes, cooked and mashed while hot
- 225 g/8 oz/2 cups plain white flour
- ½ teasp baking powder
- 2 tablesp melted bacon fat, or butter
- a little buttermilk, or fresh milk
- pinch of salt

1 Grate the raw potatoes directly into a clean cloth. Holding the cloth over a bowl, twist the ends of the cloth tightly together and wring out all the starchy liquid from the potatoes into the bowl. The wrung potatoes are placed in another bowl and covered with the hot, mashed potatoes (this prevents the grated potatoes becoming discoloured on contact with air). The liquid from the first bowl settles and the starch drops to the bottom. Carefully pour off the clear liquid at the top. Then mix the starch thoroughly with the grated and mashed potatoes. Sift the flour, baking powder and a good pinch of salt together. Mix into the potato mixture with the butter, or bacon fat. Stir in sufficient milk or buttermilk to make a firm dough. Knead as if you were making bread dough.

2 Divide into 2 pieces, roll out on a floured board, then divide into farls (triangles) or, if preferred, cut into circles with a scone-cutter. Bake at 180°C/350°F/Gas 4 for 30-40 minutes. Eat hot from the oven, split and buttered.

Champp

Serves: 4-6

Preparation: 5'

Cooking: 20'-30' depending
on the size of the potatoes

Difficulty: ●

Flavour: ●

Kcal (per serving): 345

Proteins (per serving): 9

Fats (per serving): 11

Nutritional Value: ●●

- 1 kg /2 lb 4 oz floury potatoes
- 1 large bunch (about 1 cup)
  scallions (spring onions),
  chopped
- 250 ml/8 fl oz/1 cup milk
- butter to taste
- salt and pepper

1 Steam the potatoes
(preferably in their skins).

2 Dry using an
absorbent
cloth or tea towel,
then peel.

3 Chop the scallions
and simmer in the
milk for a minute or two.
Keep warm.

4 Put the
potatoes
through a potato
ricer or mouli, or
mash thoroughly.

A row of brightly coloured houses in Kinsale, County Cork, famous for its restaurants.

Add the milk and scallion mixture, season to taste and mix thoroughly, but lightly. You may add more milk if the mixture seems dry but on no account should it become wet.

Reheat until piping hot. This can be done most conveniently in a microwave oven at a medium setting for 5-7 minutes. Place each serving on a very hot plate, make a depression in the centre and put a good knob of butter in, allowing it to melt into a little lake. Eat from the outside in, dipping each forkful into the butter.

VARIATIONS (TRADITIONAL):

Substitute 1 cup of cooked peas or broad beans (the latter skinned and finely chopped) for the scallions; or cooked chopped onion, cooked mashed parsnip, or cooked and mashed turnip (swede), or finely chopped young nettle tops (cooked in the milk until tender), or cooked chopped spinach. Chives, parsley, or wild garlic (finely chopped) are added directly to the potato rather than cooked in the milk first.

Colcannon

- 900 g/2 lb floury potatoes
- 250 ml/8 fl oz/1 cup cooked, finely chopped curly kale (for colcannon made with cabbage omit the kale and substitute 250 ml/8 fl oz/1 cup finely chopped green cabbage leaves)
- 250 ml/8 fl oz/1 cup very hot milk
- 1 bunch scallions (spring onions), finely chopped (optional)
- 4 tablesp butter

Serves: 6-8

Preparation: 15'

Cooking: 20-30' depending on size of potatoes

Difficulty: ●●

Flavour: ●

Kcal (per serving): 251

Proteins (per serving): 6

Fats (per serving): 10

Nutritional Value: ●●

Steam the potatoes until tender. Dry off by placing a clean tea-towel on top for a few minutes. Then put through a potato ricer or mouli.

1 Strip the soft kale leaf away from the stem and tougher veins. Discard the stem and veins. Shred the leaves finely. Bring a large, stainless steel pot of salted water to a furious boil, add the kale leaves and cook until just tender.

2 Drain and cool immediately under cold running water – vital if you wish to preserve the bright green colour. Drain, then squeeze out any excess liquid.

3 Place the kale in a food processor with the hot milk and process until you have a thick green "soup".

Put the scallions (if using) in a small pan with the butter and soften for just 30 seconds. While everything is still hot, lightly, but thoroughly, mix the scallions, potatoes and kale until you have a pale green "fluff". Season with salt and freshly ground black pepper, then reheat until piping hot in the microwave or (covered) in an oven. Serve with more butter.

Colcannon is eaten at Hallowe'en when the kale crop is ready, and it often has a ring put into it as a "favour". It also has the distinction of having a song dedicated to it, a song that, like the recipe itself, has two versions, one with kale and the other with cabbage.

*Did you ever eat colcannon when 'twas made
with yellow cream
And the kale and praties blended like the picture
in a dream?
Did you ever take a forkful and dip it in the lake
Of heather-flavoured butter that your mother
used to make?
Oh you did, yes you did! So did he and so did I
And the more I think about it, sure the more
I want to cry.*

Serves: 6
Preparation: 15'
Cooking: 20'
Difficulty: ●
Flavour: ●
Kcal (per serving): 227
Proteins (per serving): 7
Fats (per serving): 7
Nutritional Value: ●●

Classic Potato Soup

Melt the butter in a heavy pan and sweat the onions or leeks (with the celery if using) over a gentle heat until soft but not brown. Add the liquid and the potatoes, season with salt and freshly ground black pepper, then simmer until the potatoes are tender. Purée in a food mill or food processor, return to the pan and reheat. Check seasoning and serve hot garnished with herbs and a little cream.

VARIATIONS:
To this basic recipe you can add chopped, crisply cooked bacon, or a little leftover cooked ham, or even diced, cooked sausage. Give it a seafood flavour by adding chopped cooked prawns, scallops, mussels or clams. Ring the changes with different fresh herbs: dill, mint, marjoram, or even a little rosemary.

- 1 kg/2 ¼ lb floury potatoes, peeled (and quartered if large)
- 2 medium-sized onions, peeled and chopped, or 2 large leeks cleaned and sliced finely
- 1-2 sticks (white) celery, finely chopped (optional)
- 2 tablesp butter
- 1 ½ litres/2 ⅓ pt/6 cups half milk/half water, or poultry stock
- 3-4 tablesp chopped parsley, or chives
- a little lightly whipped cream (optional)

Potato Bread Rolls

Makes: 15 rolls

Preparation: about 2 hr (plus the time
it takes to prepare the potatoes)

Cooking: 20′

Difficulty: ●●

Flavour: ●

Kcal (per serving): 432

Proteins (per serving): 10

Fats (per serving): 12

Nutritional Value: ●●

- 110 g/4 oz floury potatoes
- 15 g/½ oz active dried yeast
- 60 g/2 oz/scant ¼ cup sugar
- 450 g/1 lb/4 cups unsifted plain white flour, warmed
- 1 teasp salt
- 60 g/2 oz butter, cut into small pieces
- 150 ml/5 fl oz/⅔ cup warm milk
- 150 ml/5 fl oz/⅔ cup warm water
- 1 medium egg, beaten
- extra milk for glazing

1 Cook the potatoes in salted water. Drain, reserving 2 tablesp of the cooking liquid. Peel the potatoes while still hot and process them with a potato ricer or food mill. Keep warm. Add the yeast and one teaspoon of sugar to the reserved lukewarm potato liquid and leave in a warm place until frothy. Meanwhile sift the flour and salt into a bowl. Rub in the butter. Make a well in the centre, then add the rest of the sugar and the warm potato and mix well. Combine the frothy yeast mixture with the warm milk and the beaten egg and about half the warm water (you may not need all of it). Knead very well until you have a smooth, softish dough (adding more water if necessary). Cover and leave in a warm place to rise; it will take about one hour to double in size.

2 Knock down on a well-floured surface, knead again and shape into rolls. Place these on greased baking trays with plenty of space between the rolls. Cover with a cloth and allow to prove for 20 minutes. Brush lightly with a little milk. Bake at 220°C/425°F/Gas 7 for 15-20 minutes until golden-brown and sounding hollow when tapped lightly on the base. The rolls are best eaten fresh but they also freeze well.

Kelly's Bakery, Wexford.

Breads and Baking

Bread is at the heart of Irish baking. Brown (wholemeal) bread raised on buttermilk and bicarbonate of soda remains the bread of the people and the one that most excites visitors to the island. In Ireland it's usually referred to as brown bread, but sometimes called wholemeal bread, in Ulster it's called wheaten bread, sometimes it's called soda bread (to distinguish it from brown, wholemeal yeast bread) and in many rural areas it is still called "brown cake" or "soda cake". This usage is a throwback to the Scandinavian word for a flattish round of bread which could be leavened or unleavened and was known as a "kake" or "kaak".

The Irish baking tradition includes a vast range of breads, scones, tarts, sweet tea breads, sweet biscuits and sweet cakes but does not include many elaborate cakes, except at festive times. It is on the plain side, but home and artisan bakers use wheat and oat flour, eggs, flavoursome Irish butter, honey, fruits and nuts to produce a range of traditional recipes that are subtle in flavour and varied in texture.

Brown (Wholemeal) Soda Bread

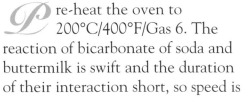

for the basic bread:
- 450 g/1 lb/3 ¾ cups wholemeal wheat flour
- 175 g/6/1 ½ oz plain white flour
- 1 teasp (generous) bicarbonate of soda
- 1 teasp salt
- about 450 ml/15 fl oz/scant 2 cups buttermilk * see following recipe

Makes: 1 loaf

Preparation: 5′

Cooking: 45′

Difficulty: ●●

Flavour : ●●

Kcal (per serving): 304

Proteins (per serving): 9

Fats (per serving): 3

Nutritional Value: ●●●

Pre-heat the oven to 200°C/400°F/Gas 6. The reaction of bicarbonate of soda and buttermilk is swift and the duration of their interaction short, so speed is of the essence if you want the bread to rise successfully. Mix the flours, salt and soda in a mixing bowl. Add only enough buttermilk to make a soft dough. Flour your hands and the work surface and knead lightly by hand, until the dough is smooth. It is important to understand that this is quite unlike making a yeast-risen dough. There is a minimum of kneading. Shape into a circle about 4 cm/1 ½ inches deep. Take a sharp, well-floured knife and cut a deep cross in the top. Place on a baking sheet and bake for 40-45 minutes. To see if it is fully cooked test by tapping the bottom and listening for a hollow sound. Cool on a rack or, if you like a soft crust, wrapped in a linen or cotton tea-cloth. Eat the same day.

VARIATIONS:

A slightly more open texture may be achieved by adding two heaped tablespoons of wheat or oat bran and enough extra liquid to absorb the bran (about 60 ml/2 fl oz/¼ cup).

ADDING GRAINS, SEEDS AND OTHER INGREDIENTS:

There are probably as many "secret" additions to the basic loaf of soda bread as there are home cooks. Pinhead oatmeal and oat flakes are common additions, so too is wheat germ. While sesame seeds and sunflower seeds probably head the list of common additions today, caraway seeds have a long history in Irish baking, particularly in seed cake. Caraway seeds are still occasionally added to soda bread as a surprise extra. Sometimes a small amount of butter, or even an egg, is added and, occasionally, a little treacle/molasses. Most people favour a coarsely ground wholewheat flour; purists prefer the wheat to be stoneground in the traditional way and there are many artisan millers in Ireland doing just that.

Making a Buttermilk Plant

Preparation: 15' plus 3'
every five days
Cooking: none
Difficulty: ●
Flavour: ●●●

Buttermilk is a byproduct of butter-making and an essential ingredient in many traditional Irish breads and baking. If you live in a country where buttermilk is not available this is a recipe for making a buttermilk plant; while it won't have exactly the same flavour, it will behave in much the same way as real buttermilk when used as a raising agent. It is far preferable to souring fresh milk with lemon juice, a practice that is sometimes recommended. The principle is similar to making a yoghurt culture at home. The plant will live indefinitely. However, if it is not fed every five days it will die off. Traditionally, you give some to a friend or neighbour and if you neglect yours they will, in turn, give you some back.

- 1 tablesp sugar
- 1 tablesp active dried yeast (not fast action)
- 600 ml/20 fl oz/ a generous 2 ½ cups fresh milk
- 125 ml/4 fl oz/½ cup boiling water

Mix the yeast with the sugar and a little warm water and leave in a warm place until it has reactivated and has a frothy top. Add boiling water to the milk and stir in the yeast mixture. Put the 'buttermilk' in a large screw top jar (at least 1 ½ litres/ 3 pints). Place in a dark, warm place. Each day give the jar a gentle shake. After about 5 days it will be ready to use. Line a colander with butter muslin through which you have poured boiling water. Place this over a large bowl. Pour the mixture through the colander. The liquid that passes through is what is used for baking. Wash the curds that remain in the colander with warm water to remove any trace of the buttermilk. Return the curds to the (re-sterilised) jar. Mix the same quantity of fresh milk and boiling water used to start your original culture and add these to the jar with the curds. Cover with the lid and place in the same dark, warm place. The second batch tends to grow faster and may be ready for use again in a couple of days, although it will keep for longer. To keep your plant alive and sweet you must repeat the process at least every five days.

White Soda Bread

- 625 g/1 lb 6 oz/5 ¼ cups plain white flour
- 1 teasp (generous) bicarbonate of soda
- 1 teasp salt
- about 450 ml/15 fl oz/ scant 2 cups buttermilk

*P*re-heat the oven to 200°C/400°F/Gas 6. Mix the flour, salt and soda in a mixing bowl. Add only enough buttermilk to make a soft dough. Flour your hands and the work surface and knead lightly by hand until the dough is smooth. Shape into a circle about 4 cm/1 ½ inches deep. Take a sharp, well-floured knife and cut a deep cross in the top. Place on a baking sheet and bake for 40-45 minutes. To see if it is fully cooked test by tapping the bottom and listening for a hollow sound. Cool on a rack or, if you like a soft crust, wrapped in a linen or cotton tea-cloth. Eat the same day.

Makes: 1 loaf

Preparation: 5'

Cooking: 40-45'

Difficulty: ●●

Flavour: ●●

Kcal (per serving): 307

Proteins (per serving): 9

Fats (per serving): 3

Nutritional Value: ●●●

VARIATIONS:

It is easy to transform plain bread into a sweet tea bread – served as a snack with butter and sometimes jam.

VARIATION:

FRUIT SODA, OR CURRANTY BREAD

Use the recipe above but with the addition of 100 g/3 ½ oz (each) of sultanas and currants. Some cooks add a tablespoon of sugar (usually brown), or honey, or treacle. This last is by far the most traditional and gives a deeper, richer colour to the bread.

VARIATION:

GRIDDLE BREAD OR SODA FARL

In most parts of Ireland white soda bread is shaped and baked just like brown soda bread. However, in Ulster it is called a "soda farl" or "griddle bread"and is usually rolled out into a flat round cake about 2 cm/¾ inch thick, then scored on both sides into four even sections called farls (quarters). The cake is then lightly dusted with flour and cooked slowly (turned once) on a griddle or a heavy frying pan until cooked through and light brown on both sides.

- 400 g/14 oz plain/3 cups white flour
- 225 g/8 oz/1 ½ cups freshly cooked, mashed floury potatoes
- 1 teasp bicarbonate of soda
- 1 teasp salt
- 500 ml/16 fl oz/2 cups buttermilk

Potato Bread

*P*re-heat the oven to 200°C/400°F/Gas 6. Mix the flour, mashed potatoes, salt and soda in a mixing bowl. Add only enough buttermilk to make a soft dough. Flour your hands and the work surface and knead lightly by hand until the dough is smooth. Shape into a circle about 4 cm/1 ½ inches deep. Take a sharp, well-floured knife and cut a deep cross in the top. Place on a baking sheet and bake for 40-45 minutes. To see if it is fully cooked, test by tapping the bottom and listening for a hollow sound. Cool on a rack or, if you like a soft crust, wrapped in a linen or cotton tea-cloth. Eat the same day.

Makes: 1 loaf
Preparation: 5'
Cooking: 40-45'
Difficulty: ●●
Flavour: ●●
Kcal (per serving): 478
Proteins (per serving): 15
Fats (per serving): 5
Nutritional Value: ●●

Baskets of bread from the Avoca shop, Suffolk Street, Dublin.

Treacle Bread

- 450 g/1 lb/4 cups plain white unsifted flour
- 1 teasp salt
- 1 teasp bicarbonate of soda
- 2 tablesp treacle/molasses
- 300-375 ml/10-12 fl oz/1 ¼-1 ½ cups buttermilk

Makes: 1 loaf or 4 farls
Preparation: 5'
Cooking: 30-35'
Difficulty: ●●
Flavour: ●●
Kcal (per serving): 224
Proteins (per serving): 6
Fats (per serving): 2
Nutritional Value: ●●

Sift the flour, salt and bicarbonate of soda into a large bowl. Take a little of the buttermilk and the treacle and warm them together, stirring until the treacle is fully dissolved. Add this mixture and enough of the plain buttermilk to the flour to make a soft dough. The ability of flour to absorb liquid varies and on this depends the amount of buttermilk needed to achieve the correct consistency.

Knead lightly. Turn the dough out onto a floured work surface and shape into a round. With a sharp knife cut a deep cross into the top, if making a loaf, or cut into four farls (triangles). Bake at 220°C/425°F/Gas 7 for 30-35 minutes or until the bread sounds hollow when lightly tapped on the base.

Treacle is a much-loved flavouring, especially in the northern counties of Ireland. Treacle is a by-product of sugar refining and can range in colour from pale gold to almost black. In Ireland and Britain the paler varieties are called "golden syrup", the darker ones "treacle".

Buttermilk Scones

- 500 g/1 lb 2 oz/4 cups plain white flour
- 1 (scant) teasp bicarbonate of soda (bread soda)
- 1 (scant) teasp baking powder
- 1 teasp salt
- 90 g/3 oz butter, cubed
- 1 egg, beaten (optional)
- about 200 ml/7 fl oz/1 scant cup buttermilk

Makes: 8-12
Preparation: 5'
Cooking: 15-20'
Difficulty: ●
Flavour: ●
Kcal (per serving): 306
Proteins (per serving): 8
Fats (per serving): 12
Nutritional Value: ●●●

Sift the flour, salt, bicarbonate of soda and baking powder together. Rub in the butter until the texture resembles breadcrumbs. Quickly and lightly mix in the egg and milk, using enough just enough liquid to make a soft dough that is puffy and easy to roll out. Knead lightly – no more than six times. Roll out to 2-2 ½ cm/¾-1 inch thick (depending on how high and moist you prefer the finished scone). For even rising, cut out the scones with a sharp fluted cutter dipped in flour, or with a very sharp knife. Transfer to a baking sheet with a palette knife. Bake immediately at 220°C/425°F/Gas 7 for 15-20 minutes, or until well risen and brown.

Scones are the great standby of the Irish country kitchen. They can be made in a few minutes and eaten warm from the oven spread with butter and accompanied with jam. Scones are eaten at all hours of the day – for breakfast, as a mid-morning snack, for afternoon tea. A plain scone can be transformed into a variety of sweet or savoury breads.

VARIATIONS: SAVOURY

Brown scones: Use half plain white and half fine-ground wholemeal flour. Cheese: Add 175 g/6 oz/1 ¼ cups grated hard cheese (extra mature Cheddar, mature Gouda, Gabriel from the West Cork Cheese Company), Parmesan. Poppy seed: Brush with milk and sprinkle poppy seeds (about 2 tablesp) over the top of the scones.
Nuts: Add 3-4 tablesp walnuts.

VARIATIONS: SWEET

Sultana: Mix in 1 tablespoon of sugar and 3 or 4 tablespoons of sultanas. Apple: Mix in 1-2 finely chopped dessert apples (peeled and cored) and a teaspoon of ground nutmeg or cinnamon. Apricot: Add about 7 moist dried apricots, finely chopped.

Oat Cakes

- 225 g/½ lb medium ground oatmeal
- 30 g/1 oz/¼ cup white flour
- ⅛ cup boiling water
- 2 tablesp melted bacon fat or butter
- a good pinch of bicarbonate of soda
- a good pinch of salt

Makes: 8

Preparation: 5'

Cooking: 45'

Difficulty: ●

Flavour: ●

Kcal (per serving): 111

Proteins (per serving): 4

Fats (per serving): 2

Nutritional Value: ●●

1 Mix the flour and the oatmeal together in a bowl. Place the boiling water in a measuring jug and mix in the fat. Add the salt and bicarbonate of soda to the water and tip it over the oatmeal and flour mixture. Mix quickly and knead lightly into a ball. The dough should be firm but not dry. The exact amount of water depends on the absorbency of the flours. Sprinkle a pastry board with more oatmeal and press the dough into a flat-ish circle. Roll out lightly and quickly into a thin cake about 18-23 cm/7-9 inches in diameter. Slide this on to a flat baking tin or pie plate and trim the edges to make them neat. Should the dough split as you roll it out just press it back together again with your fingers.

2 Cut into 8 farls or triangles. Bake at 180°C/350°F/Gas Mark 4 for about 45 minutes. The cakes should be lightly tinged with brown. Store in an airtight tin. Delicious with cheese.

Carrot and Dillisk Bread

- 30 g/1 oz dried dillisk, soaked for 5 minutes in water
- 110 g/4 oz butter, melted
- 1 large carrot, peeled and grated
- 4 medium eggs
- 60 g/2 oz/scant ¼ cup caster sugar
- a pinch of salt
- 255 g/9 oz/2 generous cups plain white, unsifted flour
- 1 ½ teasp baking powder

Makes: 1 loaf
Preparation: 10′
Cooking: 50′
Difficulty: ●
Flavour: ●●●
Kcal (per serving): 285
Proteins (per serving): 8
Fats (per serving): 8
Nutritional Value: ●●●

1 Drain the dillisk and pat dry with kitchen paper; chop finely. Brush the inside of a 900 g/2 lb loaf tin using a little of the melted butter. In a bowl, combine the remaining butter, grated carrot, eggs, sugar, dillisk and salt.

2 Sift the flour and baking powder together and fold into the mixture. Place in the loaf tin, smooth the top and bake at 200°C/400°F/Gas 6 for 50 minutes, or until a skewer inserted into the centre of the loaf comes out clean. Cool in the tin before turning out. Best eaten fresh.

Dillisk, also called "dulse" is a traditional Irish edible seaweed. It is available ready-prepared and dried. Gerry Galvin, one of Ireland's leading and most innovative chefs, created this lovely savoury bread. The dillisk lends a taste of the sea and the carrot a hint of sweetness that makes it acceptable as a teabread.

- 255 g/9 oz/1 ¼ cups raisins
- 255 g/9 oz/1 ¼ cups sultanas
- 60 g/2 oz/scant ¼ cup mixed peel (optional)
- 225 g/8 oz/1 generous cup dark cane sugar
- 500 ml/16 fl oz/2 cups Indian tea, hot, strong and black
- 350 g/12 oz/3 cups (unsifted) plain white flour
- 2 teasp baking powder
- 1 ½ teasp mixed spice
- 2 medium-sized eggs, beaten
- a little honey for the glaze
- a 20 cm/8 inch cake tin (at least 7.5 cm/3 inches deep) greased and lined with greaseproof (unwaxed) or non-stick paper
- Charms, such as a ring, to insert in the brack

Barm Brack

Preparation: 10'
  (plus soaking time overnight)
Cooking: 1 ½ hr
Difficulty: ●
Flavour: ●●●
Kcal (per serving): 582
Proteins (per serving): 10
Fats (per serving): 6
Nutritional Value: ●●●

Place the fruit, sugar and peel in a bowl and pour the hot tea over them; stir well until the sugar is dissolved, then stand overnight. The next day sift flour, baking powder and mixed spice into a bowl. Mix, alternately, some egg and some fruit into the flour, stirring thoroughly. When all the egg and fruit has been mixed in, add the ring and other charms if you are using them, making sure they are evenly distributed throughout the mix. For safety, wrap them in greaseproof paper.

Turn out the mixture into the prepared cake tin and bake at 160°C/325°F/Gas 3 for about 1 ½ hours. About 10 minutes before it is ready, brush the top of the brack with warmed honey. Return to the oven until fully cooked. Cool in the tin for 15 minutes before turning out (glazed side up) on to a rack to cool.

Eat sliced and buttered. This recipe for tea brack is moist and keeps for 4-5 days, providing it is stored in an airtight tin.

Brack, Ireland's traditional fruit bread, has been a festive dish since ancient times. It was eaten at Lughnasa (the first day of autumn and the start of the harvest), at Samhain (the first day of winter), at Imbolc (St Brigid's Day) the first day of spring and at Beltaine (the first day of summer). All Souls' Night (Hallowe'en) has supplanted the pre-Christian festival of Samhain, but it's still the night on which brack is eaten in Ireland. A ring is placed in the brack to herald marriage the following spring for whoever finds it. In some parts of the country they also insert a dried pea for spinsterhood, a bean for riches, a rag for poverty, and a piece of matchstick, which predicts that your husband will beat you! There are two versions of the origin of the name barm brack: that it comes from the Irish bairgain breac (speckled bread), or that it derives from the use of barm, yeast drawn off fermenting malt. Brack made at home is raised not with yeast but with baking powder and is called a "tea brack" because the dried fruit is soaked in tea.

Rhubarb Tart

- 1 kg/2 lb 2 oz rhubarb
- 110 g/4 oz/1 generous cup sugar
- 1 egg white, beaten until stiff

for the potato pastry:
- 225 g/8 oz/1 ½ cups cooked, floury potatoes, peeled while hot
- 225 g/8 oz/2 cups unsifted white flour
- 1 level tsp baking powder
- a pinch of salt
- 180 g/6 oz butter
- a little beaten egg

Clean and cut up the rhubarb into short lengths. Place in a pan with the sugar and simmer for about 10 minutes or until the rhubarb is barely tender. Fold in the egg white and cool. To make the pastry put the hot cooked potatoes though a potato ricer or a mouli food mill. Sift flour and baking powder together. Rub in the butter. Stir in the potatoes lightly and then add just enough beaten egg to make a firm dough. Dust a board or worktop with flour. Roll out pastry into two rounds.
Line a 20-25 cm/8-10 inch flan or tart tin with half the pastry. Spoon (or pour) the filling into the pastry case and top with the remaining pastry. Bake at 200°C/400°F/Gas 6 for 40–50 minutes until the pastry is cooked through and golden brown. Serve warm with whipped cream.

Serves: 4-6
Preparation: 15'
Cooking: 50-60'
Difficulty: ●
Flavour: ●●
Kcal (per serving): 391
Proteins (per serving): 8
Fats (per serving): 23
Nutritional Value: ●●●

In County Antrim many small bakeries used to make this dish. The origins of the word "fadge" are unknown; it is neither Gaelic nor, apparently, Ulster-Scots. It is used variously to denote a thick wheaten loaf, a potato cake baked on the griddle, or a large piece of oatcake. In homes and in the small bakeries, it described a savoury potato cake stuffed with apples.

- 500 g/1lb 2 oz floury potatoes cooked, peeled, mashed and still hot
- a good pinch of salt
- 2 tablesp butter
- 110 g/4 oz /1 cup unsifted plain, white flour
- 250 ml/8 fl oz/1 cup cooked fluffy apple purée

Apple Fadge

Serves: 4
Preparation: 15′
Cooking: 20′
Difficulty: ●●
Flavour: ●
Kcal (per serving): 255
Proteins (per serving): 5
Fats (per serving): 5
Nutritional Value: ●●

1 Mix the potatoes, flour, butter and salt together and knead lightly.

2 Divide into 4 and roll out into 4 circles. Divide the apple purée evenly between them, placing it on one side of the circle only. Fold the other side over, as if you were making a turnover, or pasty. Seal the edges well by pinching together firmly, so they do not open while cooking. Place on a baking tray and bake at 200°C/400°F/Gas 6 for about 20 minutes, or until brown and crisp. Serve hot.

These cakes are good with grilled sausages, or with pork, duck, or goose. Although Bramley apples provide the fluffiest purée, it is quite a sour apple, which you may like to sweeten with a little sugar.

Kerry Apple Cake

- 3 large cooking apples, peeled, cored and diced
- 225 g/8 oz/2 cups unsifted white flour
- 100 g/3 ½ oz butter
- 90 g/3 oz/scant ½ cup caster sugar
- 1 teasp baking powder
- ¼ teasp salt
- 1 extra-large egg, beaten
- ¼ teasp nutmeg, grated (or ground cinnamon or ground cloves)
- 3 tablesp Demerara sugar

Grease a 20 cm/8-inch cake tin with butter, then line it with greaseproof paper. Sift the flour into a bowl and rub in the butter until you have a mixture like fine breadcrumbs. Mix the salt, sugar and baking powder together in a small bowl, then stir into the flour mixture.

1 Add the chopped apples and the egg and mix to a soft dough. Turn the dough into the cake tin.

Serves: 4-8
Preparation: 15'
Cooking: 45-50'
Difficulty: ●
Flavour: ●●
Kcal (per serving): 293
Proteins (per serving): 4
Fats (per serving): 12
Nutritional Value: ●●●

2 Mix the Demerara sugar and spice and sprinkle over the top of the cake. Bake at once at 180°C/350°F/Gas 4 for about 45 minutes, or until a skewer inserted into the middle of the cake comes out clean.
Traditionally this cake is eaten hot from the oven. It can be served warm (even cold) as long as it is freshly made – just warm it gently if it is to be eaten the following day.

Cider Cake

- 110 g/4 oz butter
- 110 g/4 oz/½ cup caster sugar
- 1 teasp bicarbonate of soda
- 225 g/8 oz/2 cups unsifted self-raising white flour
- ½ teasp freshly grated nutmeg
- 2 medium eggs, beaten
- 200 ml/7 fl oz/¾ cup medium sweet cider
- 2-3 juicy eating apples, peeled, cored and sliced into wedges
- 1-2 tablesp icing sugar for the topping

Serves: 8
Preparation: 15'
Cooking: 35-40'
Difficulty: ●
Flavour: ●●
Kcal (per serving): 338
Proteins (per serving): 6
Fats (per serving): 14
Nutritional Value: ●●●

Grease a 23 cm/9 inch square, non-stick baking tin with butter.

1 Cream the butter and sugar until light and fluffy. Sift the flour, nutmeg and bicarbonate of soda together. Beat a tablespoon of the flour mix into the butter and sugar mixture followed by all the eggs. Mix in half the remaining flour.

2 Add the cider and beat in fully. Mix in the rest of the flour. Pour the mixture into the tin. Insert the apple slices into the mixture (wide side facing upwards) in an even pattern. Bake immediately at 180°C/350°F/Gas 4 for 35-45 minutes or until the top is golden, the cake begins to shrink from the sides of the tin, and the top feels springy to the touch. Allow to cool slightly in the tin before turning out carefully. Place right side up and sprinkle the top with icing sugar. This cake is also eaten as a dessert while still warm when it is served with whipped cream.

VARIATION:
Replace the apple with peeled, sliced wedges of dessert pear.

Apples are a native fruit and cider has been made in Ireland since earliest times. Ireland has a thriving cider industry and in the apple-growing areas of the island the sight of apple orchards in blossom is uplifting in springtime. Cakes made with apples are traditional on the first day of Spring – St Brigid's Day. Brigid is Ireland's second patron saint and amongst her many skills she was a renowned brewer.

Soups, Starters and Light Meals

A competitor at the annual Galway International Oyster Festival.

Light, savoury dishes are eaten at various times of the day in Ireland – in the evening, as a first course (often called a "starter"), at dinner and at lunchtime as a light meal in itself. In farming households, particularly in dairy farms where (to fit in with the milking of cows) the main meal is sometimes still taken at midday, the same range of dishes is eaten as at evening tea time. Some of these dishes are even eaten at breakfast time!

Dublin Cockle and Mussel Soup

Scrub and clean the shellfish thoroughly to get rid of any grit, sand or adhering small barnacles. Discard any that are open or do not close when tapped lightly. Place in a large, wide pot. Barely cover with salted water. Bring to the boil and when the shells have opened remove from the heat. Discard any that have not opened. It's simple to slip the flesh from the shells but do it over a bowl because you want to save any juices from the shells. Add this juice to the liquid in the pot, then use a fine strainer to strain all the cooking liquid into a bowl (this step is necessary to remove any remaining sand or grit). Melt the butter in a heavy-bottomed pan and soften the onion, garlic, celery and carrot over a gentle heat. Stir in the flour and add the shellfish liquid and the milk. Stir (or whisk) until blended and free of lumps. Simmer for about 5 minutes to cook the flour. Add the shellfish and just heat them through. Serve at once garnished with the herbs and a little cream.

Serves: 6-8
Preparation: 15'
Cooking: 10'
Difficulty: ●
Flavour: ●
Kcal (per serving): 377
Proteins (per serving): 25
Fats (per serving): 19
Nutritional Value: ●●

- about 2 dozen cockles (or clams) about 3 dozen mussels
- 3 tablesp butter
- 2 tablesp white flour
- 3 tablesp onion, peeled and very finely chopped
- 1 tablesp celery, very finely chopped
- 1 tablesp carrot, very finely chopped
- 2 cloves garlic, peeled, crushed and finely chopped (optional)
- cooking liquid from the cockles and mussels
- sufficient milk to make this up to 1.5 ltr/2 pints/6 cups liquid

for the garnish:
- 2 tablesp chopped chives
- 2 tablesp chopped parsley
- a little lightly-whipped cream (optional)

Molly Malone was a famous fishmonger in Dublin's fair city who, according to the song, "wheeled her wheelbarrow through streets broad and narrow, crying cockles and mussels alive, alive-o". When a bronze statue representing Molly was unveiled at the Trinity College end of Grafton Street, many citizens considered her rather "better-endowed" than the girl of their romantic imaginings. Dublin wits promptly christened her "the tart with the cart"! A tradition has grown up of having your photograph taken with Molly and no matter when you pass by you'll see tourists (and natives) gathered around the statue.

Nettle Soup

Serves: 6
Preparation: 10'
Cooking: 18'
Difficulty: ●
Flavour: ●●
Kcal (per serving): 148
Proteins (per serving): 5
Fats (per serving): 8
Nutritional Value: ●

- 380 g/13 oz/2 generous cups floury potatoes, peeled and cubed
- 150 g/5 oz/1 cup mild onion, peeled and finely chopped
- 3 cups (closely packed) nettle tops, washed and roughly chopped
- 2 tablesp butter (or bacon, duck, or goose fat)
- 1.5 ltr/2 ⅓ pts/6 cups chicken or turkey stock

for the garnish:
- 2 tablesp chopped fresh parsley or chives
- a little cream, lightly whipped

1 Melt the butter in a large pot and sweat the onion and potato in it, add stock and cook until tender; this will take about 10 minutes over a gentle heat.

2 Wash the nettle tops, drain them and then add them to the pot to simmer for 5 minutes only – any longer and the bright green colour fades and a rather strong taste develops. Test for tenderness. Purée the soup in a foodmill or food processor until smooth. Return to the pot and reheat. Serve garnished with a swirl of whipped cream and the chopped parsley or chives.

VARIATION: WATERCRESS SOUP
Substitute 6 cups of watercress leaves for the nettles. The traditional garnish is cubes of crisply-cooked bacon.

Nettles grow wild in Ireland. They are a traditional spring tonic, picked when the leaves are young and tender. This ancient way of flushing toxins from the system has some actual scientific basis since wild nettles are rich in iron, and are also valuable in the treatment of arthritis. Pick only the tender tops and use gloves when picking them.

- 1 tablesp butter, or olive oil
- 100 g/3 ½ oz streaky bacon, finely chopped
- 225 g/8 oz onions, finely chopped
- 2 bay leaves
- 450 g/1 lb floury potatoes, peeled and finely chopped
- 500 ml/16 fl oz/2 cups fish stock
- 300 ml/10 fl oz/1 ¼ cups milk
- 700 g/1 ½ lb mixed firm-fleshed white fish, skinned, boned, cut into bite-sized pieces
- 90 g/3 oz smoked cod or haddock, skinned, boned, cut into bite-sized pieces
- 150 ml/5 fl oz/ ⅔ cup cream
- 700 g/1 ½ lb mussels, cockles, clams, lightly cooked and shelled
- 225 g/½ lb prawns, scallops, shrimp, lightly cooked and shelled
- lots of fresh parsley and/or chives, finely chopped

Seafood Chowder

Serves: 6

Preparation: 30' (10' if you buy a ready-prepared fish chowder mixture)

Cooking: about 20'

Difficulty: ●●

Flavour: ●

Kcal (per serving): 461

Proteins (per serving): 30

Fats (per serving): 27

Nutritional Value: ●●

Melt the butter in a large pot and cook the bacon until crisp. Add onions and cook until translucent (not browned). Add potatoes, stock, bay leaves and milk and simmer until the potatoes are tender. If the potatoes have not disintegrated sufficiently to thicken the liquid to your taste use a fork to mash them into the soup. Add the fish and simmer for 2-3 minutes. Add the cream and simmer for just 30 seconds. Finally, add the shellfish. As soon as the liquid reaches simmering point again (within seconds) remove the pot from the heat. Season to taste with salt, freshly ground pepper and most of the herbs. Serve at once, hot and fresh, garnishing with the remaining herbs.

Chowder is a popular Irish seafood soup and turns up on lunchtime menus throughout the country, especially in coastal areas. Some restaurants and pubs substitute about 1/4 of the white fish content with salmon; this is done for economy reasons because farmed salmon is less expensive than wild white fish; a small amount is fine, but add too much and the strong taste of the salmon overwhelms the more delicate flavours. Chowder is usually eaten with wholemeal or crusty bread, making it something of a meal in itself.

Smoked Salmon with Wild Irish Salad

- 450 g/1 lb smoked salmon
- 1 large lemon
- freshly ground black pepper
- brown soda bread and butter

for the wild salad:
- wild leaves*
- 1 tablesp lemon juice or cider vinegar
- 3-4 tablesp olive oil
- a little sea salt and freshly ground black pepper

* Select from the following: wild sorrel, watercress, wild garlic leaves (ramsoms), dandelion leaves, young beech leaves, young hawthorn leaves, lambs lettuce, comphrey, chickweed, wild mint, thyme, marjoram, primrose flowers, borage flowers, nasturtium flowers.

Serves: 4

Preparation: 10'

Cooking: None

Difficulty: ●

Flavour: ●●

Kcal (per serving): 393

Proteins (per serving): 30

Fats (per serving): 14

Nutritional Value: ●●

Slice the salmon very thinly and lay on plates. Dress the salad leaves lightly with vinaigrette. Serve with buttered slices of brown soda bread, lemon wedges and a pepper mill; allow everyone to grind black pepper over the salmon to their taste.

Warm Clonakilty Black Pudding and Caramelised Apple Salad

- 350 g/12 oz black pudding
- 2 large, firm eating apples
- 90 g/3 fl oz runny (liquid) honey
- 175 ml/6 fl oz/¾ cup balsamic vinegar
- olive oil to taste
- mixed wild leaves or mixed salad leaves

Serves: 4-6 as a starter
Preparation: 10'
Cooking: 10'
Difficulty: ●
Flavour: ●●
Kcal (per serving): 498
Proteins (per serving): 8
Fats (per serving): 14
Nutritional Value: ●●●

*P*re-heat oven to 180°C/350°F/Gas 4. Slice pudding into rounds about 2.5 cm/1-inch thick. Place on a non-stick baking sheet and cook for 5-10 minutes. Core and peel the apples and divide into six pieces. Cook these with the honey in a heavy ovenproof pan until caramelised. Add the vinegar and place in the oven for a further five minutes. Take the apples from the pan, reserving the juice, and position around heated serving plates. For the salad dressing, quickly mix the reserved pan juices with olive oil to taste, season with a little salt and black pepper and whisk. Place salad leaves in the centre of the plate and drizzle over a little dressing. Place black pudding on top and serve at once with a little wholemeal bread.

The main ingredient in Irish black pudding is pig's blood mixed with diced pork back fat, onions, herbs, spices and oats or barley. There is wide variation in texture, flavour and shapes. The recipe for the popular Clonakilty variety (which is widely available in Ireland and abroad) is a venerable traditional one and produces a pudding that is open textured and strongly flavoured. Black pudding, often teamed with apples, is a popular first course. It also makes a great dish for a light luncheon.

Warm Bacon Salad with Wilted Leaves

■ 110-175 g/4-6 oz mixed bitter salad leaves
■ 225 g/8 oz thickly-sliced rashers of streaky bacon (preferably dry-cured), rind removed
■ 1 tablesp olive oil
■ 2-3 tablesp cider vinegar
■ freshly ground black pepper
■ shavings of Irish Gabriel or Desmond cheese from West Cork (Parmesan, or well-aged Manchego may be substituted)

Take a mixture of slightly bitter salad leaves like rocket, frisée (curly) endive, baby spinach, lambs lettuce, dandelion leaves and watercress. Wash and dry the leaves and place on serving plates.

Cut bacon into matchsticks. Heat a tablespoon of oil in a pan and cook the bacon pieces, turning frequently. Cook until the fat runs and the bacon has become lightly brown and crisp. Take pan from the heat and remove bacon on to kitchen paper. You are aiming to have about 3-4 tablespoons of bacon fat remaining; if there is too much, discard some. Add the vinegar and deglaze the pan by stirring vigorously and scraping up any crispy bits in the pan. The residual heat should concentrate the vinegar so that it reduces by about half. Use the contents of the pan to dress the leaves, tossing them to coat; the hot dressing will wilt them slightly. Sprinkle bacon over the top with shavings of cheese and eat at once with fresh white soda bread or savoury scones to mop up the juices.

Serves: 4
Preparation: 5′
Cooking: 5′
Difficulty: ●
Flavour: ●●●
Kcal (per serving): 501
Proteins (per serving): 14
Fats (per serving): 47
Nutritional Value: ●●●

Smoked Duck with Beetroot and Orange

Serves: 4 as a starter

Preparation: 5'

Cooking: 1-2 hr

Difficulty: ●

Flavour: ●●●

Kcal (per serving): 110

Proteins (per serving): 13

Fats (per serving): 1

Nutritional Value: ●●

- 175-225 g/6-8 oz smoked duck, thinly sliced
- juice of 1 orange
- 1 teasp orange zest, grated
- 4 leaves of crisp cos lettuce (or other crisp leaves)
- 425 g/1 lb beetroot

Cooked, peeled beetroot (vacuum-packed) works fine for this dish. Otherwise use small young beetroots and bake them, without peeling, until tender (1-2 hours). Peel the cooked beets and cut into large cubes (wear rubber gloves while doing this) and dress with the orange juice. On each serving plate place a cos lettuce leaf and then place the cubed beetroot in this. Sprinkle with some orange zest and serve with the smoked duck.

The Galway Oyster Festival: Held over a full week to celebrate the opening of the native oyster season in September, this great festival attracts visitors from all over the world who consume vast quantities of oysters, compete in oyster opening competitions and dance the night away at the Oyster Ball.

Oysters Irish-style

Oysters must be tightly shut. Any shell that is even slightly open should be thrown away.

Serves: 1

Preparation: 10'

Cooking: none

Difficulty: ●

Flavour: ●●●

Kcal (per serving): 268

Proteins (per serving): 14

Fats (per serving): 2

Nutritional Value: ●

- 1 dozen oysters per person is a generous portion – many are satisfied with a half-dozen.
- wholemeal soda bread and butter
- 1 pint glass of stout (Guinness, Murphy's, Beamish, or a specialist one from a micro-brewery)

1 To prise them open, place them on a work surface with the round side of the shell facing down. Wrap your left hand in a cloth. Place the oyster in your left palm, flat side uppermost. Push the point of the short, blunt oyster knife into the hinge.

2 Press the middle fingers of your left hand on to the shell. Wiggle the knife blade to left and right, then (carefully) jerk up the knife to prise the shells apart. Free the oyster from its root base and turn it best side up, taking care not to lose any of the delicious juice.

Native Irish oysters are in season from September to April (when there is an 'r' in the name of the month). Pacific oysters are now cultivated around our coast and are harvested all year round. The Irish have eaten oysters enthusiastically since the first hunter-gatherers arrived on the island nine thousand years ago; vast mounds of oyster shells have been uncovered in their kitchen middens in estuaries where oysters were plentiful.

True oyster-lovers spurn any additions and eat them straight from the shell, washed down by the juices lingering there. Sometimes a plate of sliced wholemeal soda bread and butter is served, but only to mop up the traditional pint of stout that inevitably accompanies the public devouring of oysters. There's even a very good micro-brewery in Dublin that flavours one of its stouts with oysters!

Mussels with Wine

- 48 mussels
- 1 cup dry white wine
- 2-4 cloves garlic
- 1 onion
- 1 tablesp butter
- 1 handful fresh chopped parsley
- salt and freshly ground black pepper to taste

Serves: 4
Preparation: 10'
Cooking: 2-3'
Difficulty: ●
Flavour: ●●●
Kcal (per serving): 119
Proteins (per serving): 10
Fats (per serving): 3
Nutritional Value: ●

Choose your mussels very carefully. The shells should either be tightly closed or, when given a sharp tap, should close promptly. Scrub the shells thoroughly with a hard brush and remove the beards (the tuft of fibres projecting from the shell). Place the mussels in a large pot. Traditionally they were put in with some seawater but, in fact, no liquid is necessary at this stage. Put a lid on the pot and place over heat. The mussels will steam open in the water that clings to the shells. This takes only a short time. When the shells are all open (discard any that have remained closed) remove the top half-shell. Do this carefully over the cooking pot so that any juice that escapes is caught. Put the mussels in the bottom half-shell aside into a dish over a steamer so that they are kept warm. Melt the butter in a pot and soften the finely chopped onions and garlic in it. Add the wine and allow it to bubble for a while and reduce. Now tip in the mussels and their juice and leave them just long enough to warm through. Serve them quickly sprinkled with the chopped parsley. Mussels become tough very quickly from over-cooking so do not be tempted to reduce the wine while the mussels are in the pot. Serve with lots of brown soda bread to mop up the delicious soup. Drink the rest of the wine with them or drink stout.

Main Courses

Fishing trawlers in Dingle harbour, County Kerry.

The Irish main course is substantial and traditionally composed of the centrepiece: red meat, poultry and furred or feathered game, or fish or shellfish; occasionally it may be based on eggs or cheese. In addition, potatoes, sometimes cooked in two different ways, and one or two other simply cooked vegetables or a salad are served at the same time.

Traditionally, stews and casseroles made using less expensive cuts of meats were popular for weekday, family meals. The meat, poultry or game and the vegetables are simmered together as a one-pot meal to be accompanied by potatoes. Today most Irish women work outside the home so these delicious traditional slow-cooked dishes tend to be reserved for weekend meals when everyone is at home to give a helping hand. During the week quickly prepared and cooked dishes like grilled, fried or roasted meat, game or fish, are the norm.

Irish Stew

Serves: 4-6
Preparation: 5'
Cooking: 2 ½-3 hr
Difficulty: ●
Flavour: ●
Kcal (per serving): 379
Proteins (per serving): 39
Fats (per serving): 4
Nutritional Value: ●●

- 1.4 kg/3 lb potatoes, peeled
- 1 kg/2 ½ lb stewing lamb (gigot or neck)
- 450 g/1 lb onions, chopped
- 5 tablesp fresh parsley, chopped
- 1 tablesp fresh thyme, chopped
- 250-500 ml/8-16 fl oz/1-2 cups of water
- salt and freshly ground black pepper

*P*eel the potatoes. Leave them whole unless very large. The bones in the meat and a certain amount of fat are essential to the flavour of Irish stew; the potatoes absorb a good deal of the fat and flavour of the meat. The meat is not cubed but left in fairly large pieces. When the meat is cooked enough it falls away from the bone, which then poses no hazard on the plate. Place a layer of onion on the bottom of a heavy pot or casserole. Lay the meat on this. Season with the salt and pepper and sprinkle generously with fresh parsley and much less generously with chopped fresh thyme. Layer the rest of the onions with the potatoes and finish with the rest of the herbs. The amount of water you add depends on how good the seal is between pot and lid. Bring to the boil and cover tightly. You may either simmer it gently on the hob or cook in the oven at 150°C/300°F/Gas 2 for 2 ½-3 hours.

The finished stew should be moist but not too liquid. Add a little hot water during cooking only if it appears to be getting too dry for your taste. Floury potatoes will partly dissolve into the liquid, thickening it a little; waxy potatoes will not. It's a matter of taste which you use, some people use a mixture of both. Serve with lots of chopped fresh parsley. Carrots, which should be cooked separately, are the perfect accompaniment.

This is a classic white stew. In some regions of Ireland carrots are added to the stew but purists maintain that these spoil the simple, pure flavour of the dish.

- 500 g/1 lb 2 oz bacon bits, or a streaky bacon joint, cubed
- 500 g/1 lb 2 oz good quality (meaty) Irish pork breakfast sausages
- 3 large onions, peeled, and chopped
- 1.4 kg/3 lb floury potatoes, peeled (or a mixture of floury and waxy potatoes)
- 6 tablesp fresh parsley, chopped
- freshly ground black pepper to taste
- 500 ml/16 fl oz/2 cups water

Dublin Coddle

Serves: 4

Preparation: 10'

Cooking: 2-5 hr

Difficulty: ●

Flavour: ●●

Kcal (per serving): 1487

Proteins (per serving): 36

Fats (per serving): 121

Nutritional Value: ●●●

Cut the potatoes into fairly large pieces (leave them whole if small). Chop the fresh parsley. Choose a heavy pot with a really tight-fitting lid. Put a generous layer of chopped onions on the bottom and then layer the other ingredients, giving each layer a generous twist of pepper. Add water and bring to the boil, then reduce the heat to a bare simmer. Cover very tightly. Cook for 2-5 hours. The longer and slower the cooking the better this dish will be. It cannot come to any harm providing the lid is really tight. A very low oven is best, set at 120°C/250°F/Gas ½.

Some people dislike the look of boiled sausages because they are pale and not browned. To counteract this you can lay all the sausages on top and, just before serving, set the pot under a grill to brown them. Alternatively, remove the sausages to brown separately under a hot grill just before serving. Dublin Coddle is served with buttered white soda bread and bottles of stout. You can also serve it with quickly-cooked green cabbage.

Said to have been a favourite dish of Jonathan Swift, Dean of St Patrick's Cathedral and author of the famous Gulliver's Travels, coddle is now rarely eaten outside Dublin. In the area of the inner city known as The Liberties it is a favourite Saturday night dish and also a funeral food – a humbler version of the "baked funeral meats" eaten at more elaborate funerals. The reason is purely practical: it doesn't spoil if left cooking for an extra hour or two. In Dublin, bacon bits are off-cuts from various cuts of bacon, usually a mixture of pale and smoked, which are sold cheaply in Dublin pork butcher shops specially for Dublin coddle. Normally they are a mixture of fat and lean. Streaky bacon, cut from the belly of the pig, also works well. It is usual to keep the skin on in order to add extra flavour. It is removed as you eat it and left on the plate.

Seafood Platter

- 8 fresh oysters
- 8 Dublin Bay Prawns (langoustines)
- 100 g/ 3 ½ oz peeled shrimps
- 4 scallops
- 16-32 mussels (fresh or smoked)
- 16-32 clams or cockles
- 12-16 crab toes (claws) or 100-150 g white crabmeat
- 100 g/3 ½ oz smoked salmon
- 2 fillets smoked mackerel (or smoked trout or smoked eel), peeled and halved
- barbecued salmon (hot smoked), optional
- 125 ml/4 fl oz/½ cup mayonnaise
- 2 large lemons, halved
- 4 handfuls mixed salad leaves
- wholemeal soda bread and butter

Serves: 4

Preparation: 15-20'

Cooking: 5'

Difficulty: ●●

Flavour: ●●●

Kcal (per serving): 602

Proteins (per serving): 34

Fats (per serving): 35

Nutritional Value: ●●

*O*ysters are generally eaten raw in Ireland. Prize open using an oyster knife (detailed instruction are on page 47). Serve in the half-shell.

1 Mussels, cockles and clams: Scrub and wash under running water; discard any that are cracked or fail to close when tapped. Put the mussels, cockles and clams into a large pan over a medium heat. Add 2–3 tablespoons of water. Cover with a lid and cook, shaking gently, for about five minutes. Stir halfway through so that they cook evenly. Strain and discard any that remain shut. Serve in the shell.

Prawns: Add 1 tablespoon of salt to 1.2 litres/2 pints water. Bring to a fast boil; add prawns and as soon as the water returns to a fast boil test to see if cooked. They should be firm and white. Large ones may take a further 30 seconds. Serve in the shell.

Scallops: If the fishmonger has not opened them, steam over boiling water until they just begin to open. Release the flesh with a thin knife. Wash under running water and pull away the membrane, the grey-black coloured frill and the black thread of the intestines, leaving the white flesh and the orange coral. Sear over a high heat until lightly-browned on both sides. In Ireland scallops are eaten very lightly cooked indeed, a little crusty on the outside and barely cooked within. Serve in the half shell.

Crab toes (claws) or crabmeat are usually bought ready-cooked and shelled.

2 Smoked fish: Smoked salmon is ready to serve; smoked mackerel, trout and eel are

also ready-to-eat and the only preparation necessary before placing on the platter is to peel off the skin.
Smoked mussels are sold shelled and ready to eat. Arrange seafood on large individual serving plates. Accompany with a small pot of mayonnaise, wedges of lemon, a side dish of mixed salad leaves, wholemeal soda bread and butter, a bowl in which to discard the shells and lots of paper serviettes.

- *A big platter of mixed seafood is a taste of summer in Ireland. Because it contains a large number of ingredients it is mainly eaten at one of the many restaurants and pubs that specialise in seafood. The platters are served simply, accompanied by wholemeal brown soda bread, butter, wedges of lemon, a little pot of mayonnaise and a bowl of salad leaves. Ingredients and amounts vary according to what is available. However, the platter will always include a mixture of fresh shellfish (molluscs and crustaceans) and smoked fish. Where possible the shellfish are served in the shell because eating with the hands is part of the pleasure of this dish.*

Grilled Mackerel and Gooseberry Sauce

- ■ 4 fresh mackerel, filleted and pin-bones carefully removed
- ■ a little melted butter or olive oil
- ■ 450 g/1 lb green gooseberries (a tart variety rather than a dark, purple-red dessert variety)
- ■ 3 tablesp dry white wine
- ■ 3 tablesp water
- ■ 2 tablesp sugar
- ■ 1 tablesp butter
- ■ 2 teasp fresh ginger, peeled, shredded, and finely chopped
- ■ sea salt and freshly ground black pepper

Serves: 4
Preparation: 5'
Cooking: 8'
Difficulty: ●
Flavour: ●●
Kcal (per serving): 443
Proteins (per serving): 25
Fats (per serving): 25
Nutritional Value: ●●●

Top, tail, and wash the gooseberries. Heat the sugar and water together until the sugar has dissolved. Add the gooseberries, ginger and wine and cook gently until tender. Stir in the butter and serve, as it is, hot. You may (if you prefer) purée the mixture and reheat before serving. Brush the mackerel with butter or oil, season with freshly ground pepper and sea salt, and grill for about 4 minutes (or less, depending on size) on each side; keep checking, mackerel is best slightly undercooked in the centre.

VARIATIONS:
Stuff each fish with one teaspoon of Florence fennel flesh (or leaves) very finely chopped to taste.
Stuff each fish with chopped mushroom cooked in butter and flavoured with chopped parsley and a very small amount of chopped fresh sage.

Serves: 4
Preparation: 5'
Cooking: 5-8' (depending on size of fish)
Difficulty: ●
Flavour: ●●
Kcal (per serving): 405
Proteins (per serving): 26
Fats (per serving): 24
Nutritional Value: ●●●

- 4-8 very fresh herring fillets*
- 8 heaped tablesp oatflakes
- 2 eggs, beaten
- 3 tablesp plain white flour
- 4 tablesp butter

*as herrings vary so much in size
you will have to be the judge of
how many you will need from the
fish available on the day

Fresh Herrings in Oatmeal

Wash and dry the fish. Dip each one in flour first, then in egg, then in oatflakes (press the latter on to the fish). If you have time, rest in a cool place to allow this coating to set. Heat a large frying pan, add some of the butter and heat it until it begins to foam. Add the herrings and cook on one side until the oat flakes are evenly browned but not burnt. Turn with a fish slice, add extra butter if needed, and brown on the second side. If you need to cook in batches, keep the first batch warm. Serve with wedges of lemon and grilled tomato halves. This is a classic dish; the oatmeal gives the herrings a crisp nutty flavour and keeps the flesh moist within.

Traditionally the humble herring languished at the bottom of the Irish fish hierarchy: the fish of the poor, the fish of penitence, a fish that failed to inspire love. Until the latter half of the 20th century, towns and villages all over Ireland celebrated "the whipping of the herring" on the Saturday before Easter to mark the end of the Lenten fast. A herring was threaded onto a rod and a crowd of lads, often the butchers' apprentices, whipped the herring through the streets with long willow rods. In some towns the final indignity was to drown it! However, in coastal areas, the Irish always ate herring, especially when shoals came near the shore in September. The surplus was salted and stored in barrels to eat as a flavouring for potatoes, first soaked in water overnight, then simmered in the pot with the potatoes. In more prosperous households they were "soused" in beer and vinegar, or given a coating of oatmeal and fried in butter.

Seared Fillets of Wild Irish Salmon with Watercress or Wild Sorrel Sauce

- 4×175 g/6 oz fillets of salmon
- salt and freshly ground black pepper
- 30 g/1 oz butter
- 1 teasp olive oil

for the sauce:
- 175 g/6 oz wild sorrel leaves, or watercress leaves*
- 15 g/½ oz butter
- 250 ml/8 fl oz /1 cup cream
- salt and black pepper

* Watercress and sorrel grow wild in Ireland.

Wash the sorrel leaves (or watercress), remove the stalks and chop roughly. Shake dry. Melt the butter in a pot and add the sorrel. Cook, stirring for a few minutes or until soft. Bring cream to boiling point and stir in the sorrel (to taste). Season with salt and black pepper and serve hot.

Preheat oven to 200°C/400°F/Gas 6. Season the salmon with salt and pepper. In a heavy ovenproof pan heat the butter and olive oil. When the pan is really hot sear the fillets quickly on both sides (flesh side first, skin side second) until golden brown. This should take no more than 2 minutes. Place pan in the oven and cook for a further 7-12 minutes, the time depends on the thickness of the fillets. Take care not to overcook the fish, which should be barely done and still moist in the centre. Serve hot with the sauce.

Serves: 4
Preparation: 3'
Cooking: 9-14'
Difficulty: ●
Flavour: ●●
Kcal (per serving): 563
Proteins (per serving): 40
Fats (per serving): 42
Nutritional Value: ●●●

Dublin Bay Prawns cooked in Butter and Whiskey

- 40 fresh, unshelled, raw Dublin Bay Prawns (langoustines)
- juice of one lemon
- 150 g/5 oz butter
- a handful wild garlic leaves (ransoms), chopped roughly, or 3 cloves garlic, peeled and chopped
- 2 tablesp parsley, chopped
- 30 ml/1 fl oz Irish whiskey
- 4 large wedges of lemon

Place the prawns in a wide dish. Pour the juice of the lemon over them and marinate for 20 minutes. Heat a very large frying pan. Melt the butter and when it is hot add the prawns; cook, turning and tossing them over a really high heat for 3-4 minutes or until just done. Add the chopped wild garlic leaves (or the chopped garlic) and the whiskey and the parsley; cook stirring for 1 minute. Immediately divide up between four hot serving plates. Garnish with lemon wedges and serve with wholemeal or white soda bread to mop up the juices. The pleasure of eating this is in shelling each cooked prawn as you go, dipping it in the buttery garlic and whiskey-flavoured sauce.

Serves: 4-6
Preparation: 5' plus 20' in the marinade
Cooking: 4-5'
Difficulty: ●
Flavour: ●●
Kcal (per serving): 331
Proteins (per serving): 15
Fats (per serving): 22
Nutritional Value: ●●●

Corned Beef with Cabbage and Juniper Berries

*S*oak the meat overnight in several changes of water. Place all the ingredients in a large ovenproof pot with fresh water to cover. Bring to the boil, skimming all the while. Reduce heat to a bare simmer and cover tightly. Cooked in the oven at 150°C/300°F/Gas 2, it takes between 40-60 minutes per 500 g/1lb 2 oz. Tenderness varies (depending on beast, cut and cure) so test when three-quarters of the cooking time has elapsed. (Note: If you intend to eat the meat cold, as many Irish prefer, allow it to cool in the cooking water, then remove to a plate and press lightly, either in a meat press or by covering with a plate weighed down by 2×400 g food cans. Cold, it is served with brown soda bread, salad leaves and a fruity chutney or pickled vegetables.) Shortly before the meat is cooked, shred the cabbage finely, removing the thicker parts of the stalks. Depending on the amount of cabbage you have, take some water in which the corned beef has been cooked. If you have soaked the corned beef before cooking this should not be too salty. Bring this water to a rolling-boil in a large enamelled or stainless steel pot. Add the cabbage to the boiling water and cook for 3-5 minutes; the length of time depends entirely upon the variety of cabbage. Young, fresh, spring or summer cabbage cooks extremely quickly. Savoy, or the dark, crinkly-leaved winter cabbage, takes considerably longer to become tender. When cooked, strain the cabbage thoroughly and toss quickly in butter or stir-fry it quickly in bacon fat.

A delicious and distinctive additional flavour is achieved if you stir-fry the cooked cabbage in a little olive oil in which one garlic clove, puréed with 4 dried juniper berries and a little salt, has been fried for half a minute before the cabbage is added.

- 1 ¼ kg/3 lb corned beef (silverside, topside, round, rump, or brisket which is much fattier)
- 1 onion, peeled
- 1 carrot
- 1 stick celery
- bouquet garni
- 2 cloves garlic
- some parsley stalks
- 500 ml/1 pt/2 ½ cups dry cider

for the cabbage:
- 1 large head dark green cabbage
- 500 ml/1 pint/2 ½ cups water
- 1-2 tablesp butter, unsalted
- 4 juniper berries, crushed
- 1 clove garlic, peeled and crushed

Serves: 4-6
Preparation: 10' plus overnight soaking
Cooking 2 ½-3 hr
Difficulty: ●●
Flavour: ●●
Kcal (per serving): 268
Proteins (per serving): 44
Fats (per serving): 4
Nutritional Value: ●●●

Serves: 4

Preparation: 5' plus 48 hr soaking

Cooking: 6-7 hr

Difficulty: ●●●

Flavour: ●●

Kcal (per serving): 825

Proteins (per serving): 34

Fats (per serving): 10

Nutritional Value: ●●●

Traditional Cork Crubeens

1 Mix the brine ingredients together and soak crubeens in this for 48 hours.

2 Remove from the brine and tie each pair (2) crubeens together onto a wooden dowel (this helps them keep their shape as they cook). Put into a large stock or ham pot and add the vegetables. Add vinegar and cover with water. Simmer for 6-7 hours over a gentle heat. Take the pot off the heat and allow to cool fully. Carefully lift out the double crubeen packs; remove string and dowel.

Melt the butter and mix with the dried breadcrumbs and allspice. Coat the crubeens with this. Warm the crubeens, either under a grill set at a low heat or in an oven set to 160°C/325°F/Gas 3. Cook until hot through inside and the coating is crisp and golden. Serve hot and eat with your fingers.

for the brine (enough for 4-8 crubeens):
- 10 litres/1 gallon water
- 225 ml/8 fl honey
- 200 g/7 oz brown sugar
- 1 cinnamon stick
- 4 bay leaves
- 400 g/14 oz coarse salt

for the crubeens:
- 4 crubeens (pig's hind feet)
- 2 carrots, chopped
- 2 sticks celery, chopped
- 2 small onions, chopped
- 250 ml/8 fl oz/1 cup white wine vinegar
- 110 g/4 oz butter
- 400 g/14 oz dried breadcrumbs
- ¼ teasp allspice

Beef and Stout Stew

- 800 g/1 lb 12 oz shin beef
- 2 large onions, peeled and chopped
- 3-4 carrots, peeled and sliced
- 30 g/1 oz/2 tablesp butter or beef dripping
- pot herbs (bay, parsley, thyme)
- 225 ml/8 fl oz/1 cup stout or beer
- 225 ml/8 fl oz/1 cup water
- salt and freshly ground black pepper

Melt the fat in a large frying pan and fry the onions gently until translucent and beginning to brown at the edges. Remove them with a slotted spoon and place with the carrots in the bottom of a casserole. Remove the outer membrane from the beef and any large sinews and gristle. Cut the meat into rounds about 2 cm/1 inch thick and brown quickly in the hot fat to seal them. Remove the meat from the pan and put in the casserole on top of the vegetables. Deglaze the frying pan with the stout or beer. Add this liquid to the casserole along with the water, herbs and seasoning. Cover tightly and cook slowly in a pre-heated oven at 160°C/325°F/Gas 3 for 3 hours.

Shin beef, as it cooks, produces a rich liquid. However, you may need to thicken the gravy with flour if you use a cut other than shin beef. Do this by dusting the meat pieces in seasoned flour before sealing them in the pan. It can be further enriched by adding chopped pieces of ox or lamb's kidney. The stew improves in flavour if refrigerated and reheated after a day or two. Serve with steamed floury potatoes.

Serves: 4
Preparation: 15'
Cooking: 3 hr
Difficulty: ●
Flavour: ●●
Kcal (per serving): 338
Proteins (per serving): 39
Fats (per serving): 16
Nutritional Value: ●●

In Ireland beef stews often contain stout or beer instead of, or as well as, stock or water. Like all Irish stews this one is eaten with mounds of floury potatoes, but it is also quite common for the potatoes to be cooked in the pot with the stew (added towards the end of the cooking time). In Dublin the preferred cut of meat would be shin beef because when given long, slow cooking it softens to a melting tenderness and produces thick, rich, gelatinous gravy.

Sirloin Steak with Whiskey and Cream Sauce

*H*eat a large heavy-based pan and when it is smoking hot add the oil and butter and then, after a few seconds, the steaks. Cook for 3-5 minutes on each side (the exact time depends on the thickness of the steaks and whether you like your meat cooked rare or well done). Rest the steaks in a warm place while you make the sauce. Discard excess fat from the pan. Deglaze the pan with the whiskey, allowing it to bubble up but not dry out completely. Add the cream and simmer for about 2 minutes or until the sauce thickens. Season to taste with black pepper and salt. Serve the steaks surrounded by the sauce. Garnish with sliced mushrooms cooked in a small knob of butter until their juices are reabsorbed.

Serves: 4

Preparation: 2'

Cooking: 6-12'

Difficulty: ●

Flavour: ●●

Kcal (per serving): 454

Proteins (per serving): 26

Fats (per serving): 31

Nutritional Value: ●●●

James Joyce's statue and the Spire, Dublin.

- 4 thickly-cut sirloin steaks
- 1 tablesp butter
- a few dashes of olive oil
- 60 ml/2 fl oz Irish whiskey
- 300 ml/10 fl oz/1 ¼ cups double cream
- sea salt and freshly ground black pepper

- 2 racks of spring lamb, trimmed and chined by the butcher

for the herb crust:
- 30 g/1 oz butter, melted
- 2 tablesp mild Irish mustard
- 4 tablesp olive oil
- 200 g/7 oz fine white breadcrumbs
- 2 sprigs each of rosemary, mint and a handful of parsley, finely chopped
- 1-2 cloves garlic, peeled, crushed and finely chopped
- zest of one lemon

for the pea and mint champ:
- 450 g/1 lb floury potatoes cooked, peeled and mashed (or passed though a potato ricer) while hot
- 450 g/1 lb peas, cooked
- 150 ml/5 fl oz/ ⅔ cup cream
- 45 g/1 ½ oz butter
- 2-3 tablesp fresh mint, chopped
- salt and freshly ground black pepper

Serves: 4-6

Preparation: 15'

Cooking: 20-25'

Difficulty: ●●

Flavour: ●●●

Kcal (per serving): 590

Proteins (per serving): 11

Fats (per serving): 39

Nutritional Value: ●●●

Rack of Lamb with a Herb Crust and Pea and Mint Champ

Trim excess fat from the lamb, leaving just a thin layer. Wrap the ends of the bones with foil to prevent burning. Seal the fatty side of the racks quickly in a hot pan in a little hot oil. Take up and cool.

1 Mix the butter with the mustard and spread this on the fatty side of each rack. Mix the rest of the herb crust mixture together and divide between the two racks, spreading over the fatty side and pressing it down firmly.
Roast at 180°C/350°F/Gas 4 for about 20-25 minutes for pink juicy meat. Rest before carving into cutlets.

2 Whiz peas and mint in a food processor or blender until smooth. Heat the cream and butter and stir in the peas and the mashed potatoes; beat thoroughly so that everything is well mixed. Season to taste with salt and black pepper and stir over a low heat until everything is hot through.

Roast Haunch of Venison

- 1-1 ½ kg/2-3 lb haunch of venison
- 175 g/6 oz bacon or pork fat
- 110 g/4 oz fatty streaky bacon rashers or pork dripping

for the marinade:
- 250 ml/8 fl oz/1 cup wine vinegar or cider vinegar
- 500 ml/ 16 fl oz/2 cups dry white wine
- 250 ml/8 fl oz/1 cup olive oil
- 1 large onion, peeled and sliced
- 2 carrots, peeled and sliced
- 3 large sprigs parsley
- 3 sprigs fresh thyme
- 6 crushed black peppercorns
- 6 crushed juniper berries
- 1 teasp salt

Serves: 4-6
Preparation: 20' plus 24-36 hr in the marinade
Cooking: 1 ½-2 hr depending on weight of haunch
Difficulty: ●●
Flavour: ●●
Kcal (per serving): 922
Proteins (per serving): 44
Fats (per serving): 75
Nutritional Value: ●●●

Make sure the game dealer removes the outer membrane and draws the sinews from the haunch. Cut the bacon or pork fat into thin strips and use a larding needle to insert these into the haunch. When you have finished, the haunch should have the look of a bald, blunt hedgehog.

1 Mix all the ingredients for the marinade in a large bowl and immerse the haunch completely. It needs at least 8-12 hours to marinate and if you are at all doubtful about the beast's age then give it 24-36 hours in a cool place. Turn the joint frequently in the marinade.

When you are ready to cook the meat, remove it from the marinade and dry it completely with kitchen paper. If using fatty streaky bacon, tie this around the joint so that at least the top is covered.

2 If using pork fat, render it down and paint the joint with about half of the fat. Roast on a rack in a pre-heated oven at 180°C/350°F/ Gas 4 for 20 minutes per 450g/1 lb plus 20 minutes over. With regular basting using the remaining pork fat this should produce a joint still on the rare side (which is the way venison is served in Ireland). If you prefer it well done, roast it for 30 minutes per 450 g/1 lb plus 20 minutes more. If you have a joint that weighs more than 2 kg/4 ½ lb, reduce the cooking time to 15 minutes per 450 g (for rare) and to no more than 25 minutes per 450 g for well done. Allow the joint to rest for 10-15 minutes, then remove the fatty bacon and slice the venison thinly.

A traditional garnish is croutons (thinly-sliced bread fried in a mixture of butter and olive oil until golden and crispy); seakale is a perfect vegetable accompaniment but celery or cabbage with juniper berries and garlic, or red cabbage are also favourites. Serve the venison with a dish of redcurrant or rowan jelly (*see* next recipe).

Wild deer (the native red and the introduced fallow and sitka deer and all their cross-breeds) roam the mountains of Wicklow, Kerry and other highland areas. Venison (deer meat) is so lean that it usually needs to be "larded" to prevent it drying out during roasting or grilling and large joints are usually marinated. Farmed deer is available all year round and tends to be young and tender. However, it is quite usual to marinate farmed venison for a day or two to add flavour.

Rowanberry Jelly

Makes: 4-6 jars

Preparation: 5'

Cooking: 1 hr plus straining overnight

Difficulty: ●●

Flavour: ●●

Kcal (per serving): 266

Proteins (per serving): 4

Fats (per serving): 7

Nutritional Value: ●●

*P*lace the berries and the apples (washed but not peeled) into a pot with about 5 cups of water. Bring this to the boil and boil for about 40 minutes. Strain the contents of the pot overnight through a jelly bag. Measure the juice that passes through into the bowl. You will need 450 g/1 lb of sugar for each 600 ml/1 pint of juice. Boil the juice in a heavy-bottomed pot for 10 minutes, then add the correct amount of warmed sugar. Boil again for about 10 more minutes, skimming off any scum which forms; test for setting in the usual way and when the setting is right pour the jelly into sterilised jars and seal them at once.

This jelly stores almost indefinitely as long as the seal remains intact. You can also make a jelly using this method from ripe elderberries, but flavour it with fresh, lightly bruised thyme leaves.

- 1.4 kg/3 lb ripe red rowanberries
- 900 g/2 lb cooking apples (crab-apples if possible)
- 1 ltr/32 fl oz/4 ½-5 cups water
- 450-900 g/l-2 lb sugar

In Ireland the rowan tree is called the Mountain Ash. The Celts made wine from its bright scarlet berries and used them to flavour a honey-based drink called mead. Rowanberry jelly is a traditional accompaniment to venison and game birds. In early autumn rowanberries may be gathered from wild rowan trees in upland areas.

The number of birds you need to make a main course for each person will depend on the birds chosen. Small game birds like pigeon and partridge serve one, pheasant (by far the most common) usually serves 2 people. As wild ducks come in various sizes, it's best to consider the weight when working out how many you need. A duck weighing from 750-900 g will serve two.

Pot Roasted Game Birds

Serves: 4

Preparation: 20'

Cooking: 1 ¼-1 ½ hr

Difficulty: ●●

Flavour: ●●●

Kcal (per serving): 384

Proteins (per serving): 16

Fats (per serving): 28

Nutritional Value: ●●●

- 2-4 game birds
- 30 g/1 oz butter
- 1 onion
- 1 large or two small carrots
- 1 stick celery
- 1 leek (optional)
- 1 bunch of fresh herbs like thyme, bay leaf, parsley, tied together with string
- 2-8 rashers (slices) of fatty bacon
- salt and freshly ground black pepper
- 150 ml/5 fl oz/⅔ cup red wine
- 150 ml/5 fl oz/⅔ cup game stock

for the stock:
- giblets, hearts, neck, liver (and legs of smaller birds like pigeons – if using)
- 1 small onion, peeled and sliced
- 1 small carrot, peeled and sliced
- 500 ml/16 fl oz/2 cups water
- 8 peppercorns
- 1 bay leaf
- 30 g/1 oz butter

Clean the giblets and neck under running water and dry with kitchen paper. Melt the butter in a pot, add the giblets and vegetables and fry until the vegetables are soft and beginning to brown. Add the water, bay leaf and peppercorns. Bring to simmering point and cook at that heat for about one hour. Strain, cool and remove any fat that rises to the top.

Melt the butter in a large flameproof, ovenproof casserole. Brown birds on all sides. Take up and set aside. Add the vegetables and fry for a few minutes until they begin to soften. Add the herbs and season with salt and black pepper. Lay the bacon over the breasts of the birds and set them on top of the vegetables. Pour in about half of the stock. Cover with a tightly fitting lid and simmer (or cook in a preheated oven at 165°C/325°F/Gas 3) until the birds are tender. Smaller, younger birds will take about three-quarters of an hour, older large ones up to one and a quarter hours. Take up the birds and bacon and keep warm.

Finish the sauce by adding the wine to the casserole and bubble up, scraping the bottom of the pan to incorporate any crispy bits. Add the remaining stock and boil for a minute or two. You can serve the sauce with the chopped vegetables in it or, for a more elegant presentation, strain it to remove the cooked vegetables.

Small birds like quail are served whole. Medium-sized ones can be halved by cutting through the breast and then removing the backbone with a poultry shears. Serve on warm plates with a little of the sauce. This dish is served with roasted root vegetables, like carrot, parsnips, turnip (swede) and potatoes to mop up the juices.

A variety of game birds are available in Ireland, some are common and some rare. Some are truly wild and some bred in captivity and then released into the wild for commercial shoots. The shooting seasons are strictly regulated and only game birds are shot – never songbirds. Game birds past their first flush of youth are best cooked slowly. The Irish tradition was to cook them on a bed of vegetables in a large iron pot with a well-fitting lid called a bastible; the older the bird, the longer it took to become tender. The vegetables are the normal Irish pot herb mixture: onions and/or leek, carrot and celery, with thyme, parsley and a bay leaf. The liquid is a combination of game stock made with the trimmings and, sometimes, the legs of the birds and red wine, although there is a long tradition of using stout with pigeons.

Game Pie

Serves: 6-8 as a main course
Preparation: 1 hr
Cooking: 2 hr plus cooling overnight.
Difficulty: ●●●
Flavour: ●●●
Kcal (per serving): 927
Proteins (per serving): 45
Fats (per serving): 61
Nutritional Value: ●●●

for the forcemeat:
- 700 g/1 ½ lb pork, chopped
- 225 g/8 oz bacon, chopped
- 100 g/3 ½ oz hard pork fat, chopped
- 3-4 leaves of fresh sage, finely chopped
- 2 teasp anchovy essence
- a pinch each of cloves, nutmeg, cinnamon and freshly ground black pepper

for the game filling:
- 1 kg/2 ¼ lb game meat (as available), boned and all skin removed

for the hot water crust pastry:
- 450 g/1 lb/3 ¾ cup strong white flour
- 175 g/6 oz lard
- 150 ml/5 fl oz/⅔ cup hot water
- ½ teasp salt

for the jelly:
- 300 ml/10 fl oz/1 ¼ cup game or meat stock
- 15 g/½ oz gelatine

Mince the pork, bacon and fat (or chop briefly in a food processor) to make the forcemeat. Mix in the seasonings, the anchovy essence and sage. In order to taste the forcemeat for seasoning, fry a little of the mixture until cooked, adjust seasoning of the remaining uncooked forcemeat as you feel necessary. Set aside.

A good mix of game will give the best result, especially if you have a mixture of furred and feathered. If you have only leftover pheasant you can always add colour and interest to the flavour with a few pigeon breasts, or a small wild duck, or some rabbit. If you have a lot of venison you can use some chicken or domestic duck and rabbit to balance the strong flavour. Check that all skin, gristle and bones are removed and cut the game into neat pieces. Set aside.

Make the pie crust. Lightly grease a raised pie mould, or a loose-bottomed or spring-form cake tin, about 21-22 ½ cm (8-9 inches) in diameter. Sift flour and salt into a bowl. Make a well in the centre. Bring lard and water to the boil and simmer for a few minutes. Pour the mixture into the centre of the flour, mixing well with a spoon, until it is cool enough to handle. Knead well, keeping it as warm as possible. Leave it to relax in a warm place for 30 minutes and then knead again. Reserve about one quarter for the lid.

1 Roll out the remaining pastry to fit the mould or tin, raising the sides above the level of the tin. Roll out the top and place on greaseproof paper.

2 Place half the forcemeat mixture on the bottom of the moulded pastry.

3 Lay the game pieces on top, mounding them up slightly. Finish with the rest of the forcemeat mixture.

4 Fit the pastry lid on top, pressing the edges of the top to the bottom so that it is well sealed. Cut a small hole in the top to allow steam to escape. The hole should be large enough to fit a small funnel, through which you will later pour the jelly.

Brush the top with beaten egg. Place in a roasting tin and bake in an oven preheated to 190°C/375°F/Gas 5 for 15 minutes. Then reduce the temperature to 150°C/300°F/Gas 2 and bake for a further 1 ¾ hours. Cool and place in the fridge overnight.

Next day, sprinkle the gelatine over the stock. Soak for five minutes. Bring slowly to the boil and simmer for a minute or two. Leave it to get cold but not set; it should be syrupy. Insert a small funnel in the hole in the lid of the pie and pour in the jelly, a little at a time. Continue until you can just see the level of liquid within the pie. Keep a sharp eye out to check that the jelly is not leaking through any holes in the pastry. If it is, stop pouring, plug the holes with a little softened butter and replace the pie in the fridge until the butter is set firm. Then pour in the rest of the jelly. Chill the pie for about 2 hours until the liquid is set.

Raised game pies come from the "big house" tradition where a surfeit of game needed to be used up. Its substantial crust allowed it to be transported to the next day's shoot. Today you are more likely to encounter a game terrine, which serves the same purpose of recycling pieces of leftover game and, by good fortune, the way you make the pie filling is the same. So the choice is yours, pie or terrine. What went into a game pie depended on what leftover game was available. The filling is always made up of a forcemeat (minced pork, bacon and fat), mixed game pieces and a jelly made from game stock or pig's trotters.

Spiced Slow Roasted Belly of Pork with Apple, Thyme and Cream Sauce

- about 1.5 kg/3 ½ lb pork belly, boned, skinned and trimmed of excess fat

for the stuffing:
- 1 medium onion, finely chopped
- 2-3 cloves garlic, peeled, crushed and chopped
- 90 g/3 oz butter
- 4-5 tablesp mixed fresh herbs (parsley, thyme, marjoram and a leaf of sage)
- 225 g/8 oz fresh breadcrumbs
- 1 egg, beaten

for the spiced paste:
- 2 tablesp butter, melted
- 2 tablesp fruit chutney
- salt and black pepper
- 1 tablesp lemon juice
- 2 cloves garlic, peeled, crushed and chopped
- 1 tablesp fresh thyme, chopped
- 2 tablesp Irish mustard

for the apple sauce:
- 2 medium-sized cooking apples (preferably Bramley), cored, peeled and roughly chopped
- 1 medium onion, peeled and roughly chopped
- 2 cloves garlic, peeled and crushed
- 2 sprigs thyme
- 125 ml/4 fl oz/½ cup medium-sweet white wine
- 125 ml/4 fl oz/½ cup chicken stock
- 250 ml/8 fl oz/1 cup cream

*M*ake the herb stuffing by melting the butter in a small pan and cooking the onion and garlic in it until soft. Take off the heat and stir in the herbs and breadcrumbs. When cooled (not cold), stir in the egg and season with salt and pepper.

Use a fork to prick the inner side of the meat. Combine the spiced paste ingredients.

1 Brush half the paste over the inside of the meat, then spread the stuffing over this.

2 Roll up the joint and tie firmly with cotton string.

Serves: 6-8
Preparation: 25′
Cooking: 3 hr
Difficulty: ●●
Flavour: ●●●
Kcal (per serving): 1546
Proteins (per serving): 21
Fats (per serving): 146
Nutritional Value: ●●●

Set oven to 150°C/300°F/Gas 2 and while it's heating brown the meat in a little oil. Place the meat, seam side up, on a rack in a roasting tin and roast for 3 hours in all. About half way through the roasting time, brush the meat on all sides with the remaining paste and then replace, seam side down, on the rack.

Make the apple and cream sauce by placing all the ingredients in a pot and simmering them for about 15 minutes. Take out the thyme stalks and whiz the sauce in a food processor or blender. Strain. If it appears too thick you may add a little extra stock. Serve hot with the meat cut into reasonably thick slices.

Jerpoint Abbey in County Kilkenny, which dates from the 12th century.

Chicken Breasts stuffed with Apples and White Pudding and baked in Cider

*M*ix the white pudding, cooking apple, breadcrumbs, parsley and chives together and moisten with just a tablespoon or two of cider so that the mixture holds together. Partially lift the skin off the breasts and push equal amounts of the stuffing into the pockets formed. (Or make a cut ¾ way through the chicken breasts and insert the stuffing as shown in the picture). Place the chicken breasts in one layer in a roasting tin just large enough to fit them snugly. Season the top with salt and freshly ground black pepper. Pour the cider and chicken stock round them and bake, covered, at 180°C/350°F/

Gas 4 for 25-30 minutes. Uncover and continue cooking for a further 15-20 minutes until the chicken is cooked through and the skin crisply browned. Remove the chicken breasts and keep warm. Add the cream to the pan juices and bring to boiling point; simmer until the liquid is reduced by half and the sauce is pleasingly thick. Check seasoning. Serve the chicken surrounded by a little sauce, garnished with wedges of red-skinned dessert apples.

NOTE: You can substitute black pudding for the white pudding if you wish.

Serves:	4
Preparation:	15'
Cooking:	40-50'
Difficulty:	●●
Flavour:	●●
Kcal (per serving):	644
Proteins (per serving):	34
Fats (per serving):	36
Nutritional Value:	●●●

- 4 breasts of chicken, complete with skin
- 100 g/3 ½ oz open-textured white pudding, crumbled
- 1 cooking apple (Bramley), peeled, cored and finely chopped
- 60 g/2 oz fresh breadcrumbs
- 2 tablesp fresh parsley, chopped
- 1 tablesp chives, chopped
- 250 ml/8 fl oz/1 cup medium dry Irish cider
- 90 ml/3 fl oz/⅜ cup chicken stock
- 60 ml/2 fl oz/¼ cup double cream
- salt and freshly ground black pepper

for the garnish:
- 2 red-skinned dessert apples, cored and sliced into thin wedges

Desserts

Hook Head lighthouse, County Wexford,
the oldest in Europe.

The Irish like to finish a meal with something sweet. In the home fresh fruit and cream, baked fruit tarts served with cream or ice cream, a slice of cake, or a tea bread, tend to be more popular than "fancy" light desserts. But there are some favourites, many based on rich Irish cream and frequently flavoured with whiskey-based liqueurs.

Another popular way to finish a meal is with a selection of Irish cheeses accompanied by biscuits, traditional oatcakes and fruit.

Carrageen Jelly (Blancmange)

- 15 g/½ oz dried carrageen moss
- 700 ml/23 fl oz/3 cups full-fat fresh milk
- 1 tablesp sugar (or to taste)
- 1 vanilla pod, or the thin peel of one lemon

Serves: 4

Preparation: 2'

Cooking: 10' plus cooling and chilling time

Difficulty: ●

Flavour: ●

Kcal (per serving): 121

Proteins (per serving): 5

Fats (per serving): 6

Nutritional Value: ●

1 Work the dried carrageen very gently under cold running water until it becomes just soft and pliable. Put it in a pan with the milk, a vanilla pod (or the lemon peel) and sugar. Simmer over a medium heat until virtually all the carrageen has dissolved.

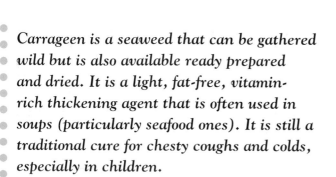

2 Strain into a bowl to remove any small pieces of tougher seaweed that remain. Pour the strained liquid into small ramekins or into a large decorative jelly mould and allow to set in a cool place.

Serve with seasonal fruit: strawberries, raspberries, or a mixed soft fruit compote of redcurrants, blackcurrants, white currants, blackberries, loganberries (or other similar soft fruits). A crisp (oaten or shortbread) biscuit provides a pleasant contrast in texture.

Carrageen is a seaweed that can be gathered wild but is also available ready prepared and dried. It is a light, fat-free, vitamin-rich thickening agent that is often used in soups (particularly seafood ones). It is still a traditional cure for chesty coughs and colds, especially in children.

Irish Mist Souffle

■ 90 g/3 oz butter
■ 60 g/2 oz flour
■ 300 ml/10 fl oz/1 ¼ cups milk
■ 60 g/2 oz caster sugar
■ 4 large eggs (separated)
■ 3×15 ml tablesp Irish Mist liqueur

Beat the egg whites until stiff, adding the sugar as if you were making meringues. Make a roux with the butter and flour, stirring over a gentle heat for 2 minutes. Add in the milk and stir to mix it through. Cook gently for 5 minutes. Add and stir in the Irish Mist liqueur. Allow to cool slightly, then beat in the egg yolks, one at a time. Stir in 1 tablespoon of the stiffly beaten egg whites, then fold in the remainder. Turn out gently into a two-pint souffle dish. Bake at once for 40-45 minutes in a pre-heated oven at 190°C/375°F/Gas 5.

Serve with a warm raspberry, blackberry, or blueberry purée. The raspberries need no sweetening. To prepare the purée, just pass the fruit through a mouli (food mill) to remove the seeds. Blackberries and blueberries need roughly 110 g/¼ lb of sugar for each 450 g/1lb of fruit. Stew the fruit and the sugar together gently until the fruit is soft; then work the mixture through the mouli/sieve to remove the skins and seeds. These sauces can all be prepared in advance and re-heated to serve with the souffle.

Serves: 4
Preparation: 10'
Cooking: 40-45'
Difficulty: ●●
Flavour: ●●●
Kcal (per serving): 679
Proteins (per serving): 17
Fats (per serving): 33
Nutritional Value: ●●●

- 700 g/1 ½ lb/3 ½ cups caster sugar
- 2 ⅓ ltrs/4 pts/9 ¼ cups water
- 600 ml/20 fl oz/2 ½ cups Bailey's (or other) Irish Cream liqueur
- borage flowers (optional)

Bailey's Irish Cream Water Ice

Serves: 8

Preparation: a few minutes, plus freezing time

Cooking: none

Difficulty: ●

Flavour: ●●●

Kcal (per serving): 288

Proteins (per serving): 1

Fats (per serving): 0

Nutritional Value: ●●●

Make a syrup of the sugar and water by boiling together until it leaves a sticky film on the back of a metal spoon. Allow it to cool. Mix in the cream liqueur. Pour into your ice-cream maker and process until frozen. Serve slightly softened in glasses decorated with blue borage flowers. Do not keep for even a single day or the liqueur's flavour and aroma will be lost.

Bailey's Irish Cream liqueur was the first of its kind. Now there are half a dozen others, but Baileys is the most widely available and the world's fifteenth largest spirit brand. As well as being a favourite drink it is also used in desserts, including cheesecake and trifle and in sweet sauces.

Serves: 4

Preparation: 15' plus chilling time

Cooking: 2'

Difficulty: ●

Flavour: ●●

Kcal (per serving): 248

Proteins (per serving): 5

Fats (per serving): 17

Nutritional Value: ●●●

- 300 g/10 oz fraughans (or blueberries)
- 90 g/3 oz/scant ½ cup caster sugar, or to taste
- juice of 1 lemon
- 125 ml/4 fl oz/½ cup double cream
- 60 ml/2 fl oz fresh cream cheese
- 1-2 tablesp water

Fraughan Fool

Lughnasa was the ancient Celtic festival of Lugh, the pagan sun god of light and genius. Celebrated in early August, it marked the beginning of the harvest and the ripening of the fruits of the earth. Fraughans (wild blueberries) were one of the first wild fruits to ripen in Ireland. The tradition was to climb a high mountain, pick fraughans and light a Lughnasa fire in tribute to the sun god who made the harvest possible. Christianity overcame the sun god Lugh, but the tradition of young people gathering on a local mountain for feasting, games, trials of strength, courting and wild dancing lived on. In the past few years fraughan festivals have been revived in mountainous parts of Ireland. Fraughans, which are similar to cultivated blueberries, are a secretive berry; they hide beneath the leaves of the low-growing wild plant.

Place the fraughans in a pot with the water and cook over a gentle heat until just soft. Reserve a few of the whole berries. Purée the berries with the sugar in a food processor. Pass the purée through a fine sieve; the resulting purée should be thick. Add the lemon juice, taste, and adjust to taste with sugar. Whisk the cream until it holds soft peaks, then gently whisk in the fresh cream cheese.

Fold two-thirds of the fraughan purée into this mixture. Add the reserved berries to the remaining purée and divide most of this into four wine glasses. Divide half of the cream, cheese and fraughan mixture between the glasses. Spoon a thin layer of the remaining fraughan purée on top of this. Finish with another layer of the creamy mixture. Chill. Serve with crisp oat or hazelnut biscuits.

Blackberry and Apple Crumble

for the filling:
- 700 g/1 ½ lb cooking apples (preferably Bramley)
- 250 g/9 oz blackberries
- 110 g/4 oz/½ cup sugar (or to taste)
- a few whole cloves, or ½ teasp freshly ground nutmeg

for the crumble:
- 110 g/4 oz/1 cup unsifted plain white flour
- 60 g/2 oz/⅔ cup oatflakes
- 90 g/3 oz butter, chopped
- 100 g/3 ½ oz/scant ½ cup light brown sugar

Serves: 4-6
Preparation: 10'
Cooking: 40-45'
Difficulty: ●
Flavour: ●●
Kcal (per serving): 515
Proteins (per serving): 4
Fats (per serving): 36
Nutritional Value: ●●●

*P*eel, core and slice the apples into wedges. Place in an oval or rectangular pie dish with the blackberries. Sprinkle the sugar and spice on top. If you have a sweet tooth use the full amount. Rub the butter into the flour. Add the sugar and oatflakes and mix well, pressing it lightly together. Spread this evenly over the fruit. Bake at 180°C/350°F/Gas 4 for 40-45 minutes or until the crumble is golden-brown and the fruit tender. Serve hot with whipped cream.

Instead of apples you may substitute rhubarb, plums, a combination of blackberries and apple, or gooseberries.

ALTERNATIVE CRUMBLE TOPPING:

- 175 g/6 oz/1 ½ cups unsifted plain flour
- 90 g/3 oz butter
- 90 g/3 oz/scant ½ cup Demerara sugar
- 60 g/2 oz/½ cup walnuts, chopped

Rub the butter into the flour and then mix in the sugar and chopped walnuts. Spread on top of filling and press down lightly.

Irish Farmhouse Cheeses

Young Irish dancers in traditional costume.

Cheeses formed a substantial part of the Irish diet until the close of the seventeenth century. Gradually, historical and economic factors caused a slow but inexorable decline in cheese eating and cheese making in Ireland. A century later, to use up milk surpluses, agricultural co-operatives began to manufacture and market "creamery" cheeses with great success, exporting mainly a cheddar-type cheese all over the world. About thirty-forty years ago a new generation of young farmhouse cheesemakers began a revival of this ancient Irish tradition. Although these new cheesemakers took their craft skills from mainland Europe, what astounds European visitors to this day is the fact that all our farmhouse cheeses are unique to their maker. But common to all of them is the high quality of Irish milk. Our climate allows cows, goats, and sheep to be out on green, well-watered grass for nine months of the year and to feed on natural grass fodder in winter. Many artisan cheesemakers farm in regions renowned for the abun-

dance and variety of the natural herbage; this, together with the personality of the cheesemaker, is what makes each farmhouse cheese unique. Today there are over eighty farmhouse cheesemakers. Many of these unique cheeses are exported and Irish farmhouse cheeses can now be found in speciality food shops all over the world.

A simple cheeseboard is the ideal way to appreciate the range and individuality of Irish farmhouse cheeses. Choose at least three cheeses offering a variety of tastes, textures, strengths, and colour. Offer them in order of strength, the mildest first, then going towards the strongest. The following suggestions are just some of the many possible combinations that will allow you to enjoy the wonderful world of Irish farmhouse cheeses.

An Irish cheeseboard is served accompanied by traditional oatcakes, plain water biscuits, or wholemeal bread. Sometimes fruits like apples, pears, grapes, or even crisp celery sticks, are offered on the side.

1. **MINE GABHAR** from Croghan Goat Farm. A natural rind cheese, silky, slightly sweet, with oaky, herbal flavours. **OISÍN** is an organic Gouda-style cheese which, when well aged, packs a powerful flavour. **ARDRAHAN** is a rustic, golden-brown washed rind, semi-firm cheese whose earthy, smoky flavour grows more robust as it ages. **DESMOND** and **GABRIEL** from the West Cork Cheese Company are made in the Swiss alpage-style; **DESMOND** is the more intense, with spicy flavours balanced by floral elements; **GABRIEL**, though more delicate, is still intense, but sweeter, subtler.

2. **KNOCKALARA** is a fresh, moist sheep's cheese, a delicate taste with hints of citrus and herbs. **CORLEGGY** is a natural rind goat's cheese with a firm smooth texture and rich multi-layered flavours. **CASHEL BLUE** has its own buttery-sweet tang. Eaten at about 4 months, it becomes a rich yellow and turns buttery. **MILLEENS** has a mottled peach or sometimes fiery orange washed rind. It develops from semi-firm to flowing cream with a complex flavour of herbs with a spicy tang.

3. **BOILIE** Goat's Cheese from Ryefield Farm is soft, fresh and aromatic. **DILLISKUS** is a hard cheese, packed with taste that is not overwhelmed by the flavour of the dillisk (a seaweed traditional to Irish food culture). **CRATLOE HILLS GOLD** is a sheep's milk cheese which, when well aged, has a dry texture and a robust fudge flavour. **CROZIER BLUE**, a sheep's milk cheese from the makers of **CASHEL BLUE**, has a pronounced, smooth flavour and a thick, buttery texture. **WICKLOW BAWN** is a fresh tasting creamy Camembert-type. When ripe it has a smooth, robust flavour with a tangy finish. **DURRUS** is a washed rind cheese. It has an earthy flavour and a velvety, moist texture. **GUBEEN** is a washed rind cheese which if eaten well-aged develops a scented mushroom flavour to compliment the younger oaky flavour and moist texture of the cheese.

Festive Recipes

The royal blue dining room, Bantry House, County Cork.

In Ireland the spirit of hospitality is deeply ingrained and there is nothing Irish people enjoy more than to celebrate a festive or feast day with a gathering of family and friends. Festive meals are more elaborate than those served during the rest of the year and traditional special dishes or foods unique to the occasion will be on the menu. There are many special days in the Irish calendar.

St Patrick's Day (being the National Holiday) inspires a number of drinks as well as food, Christmas is the most important festival, when families and friends from abroad gather together and enjoy a traditional Christmas dinner – roast stuffed turkey or goose, baked ham, Christmas pudding, mince pies, and finish with the incredibly rich and elaborately decorated Christmas cake (which gives rise to competitive baking and visitors are expected to pass judgment on its merits). At Easter, delicate spring lamb is the central dish (while the children feast on chocolate Easter eggs). Hallowe'en is another festival where special dishes feature, particularly Barm Brack and colcannon, which traditionally contain a ring and other favours.

Irish Whiskey-Fed Christmas Cake

- 450 g/1 lb/3 cups currants
- 175 g/6 oz/1 cup sultanas
- 175 g/6 oz/1 cup raisins
- 60 g/2 oz/⅓ cup glacé cherries, washed and chopped
- 60 g/2 oz/⅓ cup mixed citrus peel, finely chopped
- 225 g/8 oz/2 cups unsifted plain white flour
- 1 teasp ground cinnamon
- 1 teasp ground nutmeg
- 1 teasp ground dry ginger
- 60 g/2 oz/½ cup chopped almonds
- 225 g/8 oz/1 generous cup dark brown sugar
- 1 tablesp treacle, warmed
- 225 g/8 oz unsalted butter
- 3 large eggs
- grated zest of 1 unwaxed lemon
- grated zest of 1 unwaxed orange
- 3 tablesp Irish whiskey (and more to feed the cake)

for the traditional icings:
Almond icing (marzipan):
- 225 g/8 oz almonds/2 ½ cups, ground
- 110 g/4 oz/1 cup icing sugar
- 110 g/4 oz/1 cup caster sugar
- 2 teasp lemon juice
- 1 medium-sized egg, beaten

for the glaze:
- 3 tablsp redcurrant jelly
- 3 tablsp water

(Note: 500 g/1lb 2 oz ready-prepared almond icing (marzipan) may be substituted for this icing).

Royal icing:
- 2 medium-sized egg whites
- 450 g/1 lb/4 cups icing sugar
- ½ teasp lemon juice
- 1 teasp glycerine

for the alternative fruit and nut topping:
- 90 g/3 oz/½ cup whole glacé cherries (both red and green)
- 90 g/3 oz/ cup whole nuts (brazil and walnuts)

for the glaze:
- 250 ml/8 fl oz/1 cup Irish cider
- 110 g/4 oz/generous ½ cup caster sugar

For best results choose high quality dried fruit (sulphur-free, if possible). The night before baking the cake put all the dried fruit into a bowl and sprinkle it with the whiskey; cover and leave to absorb the flavour.

Grease a 20 cm/8-inch round (or an 18 cm/7-inch square) loose-based, deep, cake tin and line with greaseproof paper. Sift the flour and spices together into a bowl.

1 Cream the butter and sugar together until very light, pale and fluffy. Beat one tablespoon of flour into the creamed butter and sugar, then beat in the eggs, one tablespoon at a time. Do this very thoroughly and, if the mixture appears to be splitting or curdling, add a little flour before the next addition of egg. Fold in the flour (no beating this time). Now stir in all the remaining ingredients. You will have a stiff mixture (if it seems too stiff add a little cider). It is traditional that members of the household, especially the children, make a wish while stirring the cake, and now is the time for them to give the cake a final stir. Place the mixture in the cake tin, spreading it out and making a depression in the centre (gently) with the back of a spoon.

The Great Hall, Bunratty Castle, County Clare.

Traditionally, this cake is double-iced, first with almond icing (marzipan) then with royal icing and then decorated with sprigs of holly leaves and berries, or ready-made Christmas figures such as Santa Claus. The same cake, with different decorations, is used for weddings and christenings. Alternatively, the cake may be topped with fruit and nuts in a decorative pattern.

Serves: 12-16

Preparation: 45'
  plus maturing time 6-8 weeks

Cooking: 4-4 ¾ hr

Difficulty: ●●●

Flavour: ●●●

Kcal (per serving): 560

Proteins (per serving): 4

Fats (per serving): 9

Nutritional Value: ●●●

Irish whiskey by making several holes in the top with a thin skewer or darning needle and dribbling in teaspoons of whiskey. Allow it to soak in, then re-wrap. At the next feeding time, do the bottom; and then do the sides.

ICING THE CAKE:

2 Three days before Christmas begin the icing. First, to help the almond to adhere to the cake, the glaze must be applied. Melt the redcurrant jelly in an equal quantity of water and brush half of it on the top of the cake.

3 To make the almond icing (marzipan), mix together the sugar and ground almonds,

It is traditional to tie a band of brown paper around the tin (an effort to prevent scorching) but few people bother. However, you should have a double-thickness sheet of greaseproof paper at the ready to place on the top of the cake if the top is becoming too browned. Bake at 130°C/275°F/Gas 1 on a shelf below the middle of the oven for 4 ¼-4 ¾ hours. Do not on any account open the door of the oven in the early stages. After about 3 hours it is safe to check it at odd intervals and cover the top if it seems necessary. But close the oven door gently! The cake is done when you cannot hear a trace of a sizzling sound and a skewer inserted in the centre comes out clean. Cool in the tin. Turn out, remove the paper, and wrap in a double thickness of fresh paper and store in a tin to mature for 6-8 weeks. Feed, at intervals, with

adding just enough egg to give a soft consistency. Knead until the paste is soft and pliable. Dust the working surface with icing sugar. Take about one-third of the almond icing and roll out to the size of the cake. Place the cake, glazed side down, on the icing and press firmly. Trim off any excess and turn right side up. Roll the remaining icing into a long strip (the circumference is about three times the diameter). Brush the sides with the remaining glaze. Roll the side of the cake along the strip, pressing the icing into the cake as you roll. Trim edges and rub lightly until you have a smooth finish. Dry in a cool place overnight.

4 Make the royal icing by whisking egg whites until frothy. Stir in half the sugar until dissolved. Whisk in remaining sugar, a little at a time. Add lemon juice and glycerine and continue whisking until the mixture is light, fluffy and forms peaks. Cover the bowl with a damp cloth or cling-wrap and stand for one hour before using. Stand cake on a turntable and spread icing with a palette knife, pressing out any air bubbles that form. It is usual to pipe rosettes round the top edge of the cake. However, before you do this the icing must be allowed to dry for 24 hours in a cool, dry place (ideally no hotter than 18°C). Make sure the icing is fully dry before you decorate it with holly or any readymade Christmas decorations.

THE ALTERNATIVE FRUIT AND NUT TOPPING
A day or so before Christmas place the sugar and cider together in a pot, bring to the boil stirring, then reduce the heat and simmer until the liquid is reduced to about five tablespoons. Brush about half of this on the cake top; place the cherries and nuts in rows (or whatever pattern pleases you) and then use the remaining glaze to brush the fruit and nuts.

Spiced Beef

Serves: 6-10
Preparation: 15' plus 2' every day for 18 days
Cooking: 3 ½-5 hr
Difficulty: ●●●
Flavour: ●●●
Kcal (per serving): 267
Proteins (per serving): 50
Fats (per serving): 2
Nutritional Value: ●

1 Spice the beef by mixing the salt and saltpetre and rub some of it into the meat, making sure it gets well into all the hollows and cracks. Place in a glass or other non-metallic bowl and keep covered in the fridge or another really cool place.

Repeat this procedure every day for 4 days. Next grind the whole spices and mix them with the sugar, cloves and bay leaves. Rub this mixture into the beef and place in a clean dish. Store in the fridge. Every second day for the following 10-14 days, turn the joint over and rub in the spices that adhere to the meat.

2 Before cooking, tie a bunch of thyme and a few bay leaves to the joint. Place it in a pot just large enough to fit the meat. Add an onion stuck with the cloves, a carrot, a stick of celery and a dozen whole peppercorns. Cover with cold water (mixed, if you wish, with a bottle of stout, for a distinctive flavour). Bring to simmering point, cover tightly and cook in a low oven set to 140°C/275°F/ Gas 1 for about 5 hours. If you prefer, simmer it very gently for about 3 ½ hours on the hob. It should be quite soft and tender when fully cooked.

3 Spiced beef can be eaten hot but it is more usual to serve it cold. To do this, allow it to cool in the cooking liquid for about 2 hours. Remove and wrap in greaseproof paper, then press it lightly with weights while stored in the fridge. To serve, slice it very thinly with a very sharp knife. It is often served as finger food on thinly-sliced wholemeal bread spread with a fruit chutney, and with chopped pickles (sweet and sour pears, sweet pickled onions, or piccalilli are good), or as a plated dish with a green salad, or a celery and walnut salad, a accompanied by crusty white bread and butter.

NOTE: It is important to weigh the ingredients for this recipe very carefully.

■ about 2 kg/4 ½ lb beef (silverside, topside, round, rump, or brisket)

for spicing (about 3 weeks):
■ 15 g/½ oz saltpetre
■ 225 g/8 oz sea salt
■ 30 g/1 oz allspice
■ 30 g/1 oz whole black peppercorns
■ 90 g/3 oz dark brown sugar
■ 12 dried juniper berries (crushed)
■ a big pinch of ground cloves
■ 3 bay leaves

for cooking:
■ a bunch of fresh thyme
■ 3 bay leaves
■ 1 onion, studded with whole cloves
■ 1 carrot
■ 1 stick celery
■ 12 whole peppercorns

Spices have been imported into Ireland since earliest times but were scarce and expensive, so this dish was always reserved for a festive feast, particularly at Christmas. It's a tradition that lives on today and no Irish Christmas cold table is complete without spiced beef.

- about 450 g/1 lb shortcrust pastry

for the mincemeat:
- 700 g/1 ½ lb/4 cups dried fruit (equal proportions of sultanas, raisins and currants)
- 110 g/4 oz/¾ cup mixed citrus peel (optional)
- 225 g/8 oz/generous 1 cup moist dark-brown sugar (muscovado)
- 110 g/4 oz/1 cup beef suet, shredded
- 60 g/2 oz/⅔ cup ground nuts (hazel or almonds)
- 1 large (tart) cooking apple, peeled, cored and finely chopped
- 1 teasp nutmeg, grated
- ½ teasp allspice, ground
- ½ teasp cinnamon, ground
- 1 lemon, zest and juice
- 125 ml/4 fl oz/½ cup Irish whiskey

Makes about 2×450 g/1 lb jars of mincemeat (enough for 12 pies).

Serves: 12
Preparation: 20' plus maturing time of 2 weeks for mincemeat
Cooking: 20'
Difficulty: ●●
Flavour: ●●●
Kcal (per serving): 526
Proteins (per serving): 3
Fats (per serving):12
Nutritional Value: ●●●

Mince Pies with Irish Whiskey

Make the filling two weeks in advance to allow the flavours to develop. In a large mixing bowl stir all the ingredients together until well mixed. Cover and leave in a cool place for 24 hours. Mix well again before potting into clean preserving jars. Cover tightly and store in a cool, dark place.

To make the pies, lightly grease the base of a shallow 12-space bun tin. Roll out the pastry and use a 9 cm/3 ½-inch pastry cutter (or whatever size fits your bun tin) to cut out 24 rounds. Place one in each of the twelve bun tins then fill it with about a heaped teaspoon of the mincemeat. Dampen the edges of each pastry case before placing the remaining twelve pastries on top as lids. Press the edges together to seal firmly. Bake at 220°C/425°F/Gas 7 for about 20 minutes or until golden-brown. Remove the pies from the tin carefully and place them to cool on a wire rack. Dust with icing sugar and serve while still warm. They are usually served with a little whipped cream.

- joint of ham (of your choice)
- 1 onion, peeled
- 1 large carrot
- 2 celery stalks
- 1 bay leaf
- 8 whole black peppercorns

for the glaze:
- 1-2 whole cloves
- 250 ml/8 fl oz/1 cup freshly squeezed orange juice
- 2-3 tablesp Demerara sugar
- 1 teasp mustard powder

for the sauce:
- 2 Bramley cooking apples, peeled, cored and chopped
- 300 ml/10 fl oz dry cider
- 1 teasp sugar, or more to taste
- 1 tablesp wholegrain Irish mustard, or Dijon mustard
- 2 teasp butter

Serves: 4-16 depending on size of joint.
Preparation: 5' plus soaking time
Cooking: 1 ½-5 hr depending on size of joint.
Difficulty: ●●
Flavour: ●●
Kcal (per serving): 266
Proteins (per serving): 29
Fats (per serving):10
Nutritional Value: ●●

Baked Ham with Cider, Mustard and Apple Sauce

Soak the ham for 12 hours in two changes of water. Place in a large pot, add vegetables, bay leaf and peppercorns and cover with cold water. Bring slowly to simmering point, cover, and barely simmer for 25 minutes for each 450 g/1 lb (for joints over 3.5 kg/8 lb, allow 20 minutes per 450 g/1 lb). Leave to cool a little in its cooking liquid off the heat. Lift out and remove the skin from the ham, leaving the fat. With a sharp knife cut a lattice pattern in the fat. Mix sugar and dry mustard powder and press evenly all over the joint. Press back any coating that falls off. Stick a clove into the cuts where the lines cross. Heat oven to 220°C/425°F/Gas 7. Place the ham in a roasting tin surrounded by the orange juice. Bake for about 20 minutes or until the sugar has slightly caramelised.

Cook the apple in the cider and sugar until soft. Beat with a wooden spoon until smooth. Stir in the mustard and butter and season to taste. Serve hot. You may, if you wish make the sauce into a froth by whisking with an electric mixer just before serving.

Hallowe'en Pudding with Egg Custard

- 60 g/2 oz/½ cup unsifted white flour
- 100 g /3 ½ oz butter, cut into small dice
- 110 g/4 oz/1 cup wholemeal breadcrumbs
- ½ teasp bicarbonate of soda
- 1 teasp mixed spice
- ½ teasp salt
- 60 g/2 oz/¼ cup caster sugar
- 225 g/8 oz/1 ¼ cups mixed dried fruit
- 1 tablesp treacle
- 175 ml/6 fl oz/¾ cup buttermilk

for the custard:
- 5 egg yolks
- 60 g/2 oz/¼ cup caster sugar
- ½ a vanilla pod, or 1 teasp vanilla essence
- 500 ml/16 fl oz/2 cups full fat milk or single (light) cream
- 60 ml/2 fl oz Irish whiskey or to taste

1 Sift the flour into a mixing bowl with the butter. Rub the butter into the flour until the mixture resembles breadcrumbs. Sift the soda, mixed spice and salt together and mix thoroughly into the flour mixture. Add all the other ingredients, using just enough buttermilk to give a soft but not sloppy mixture. Grease a 1 litre/2 lb/2 pint pudding bowl with butter (it should be large enough to allow the mixture to expand).

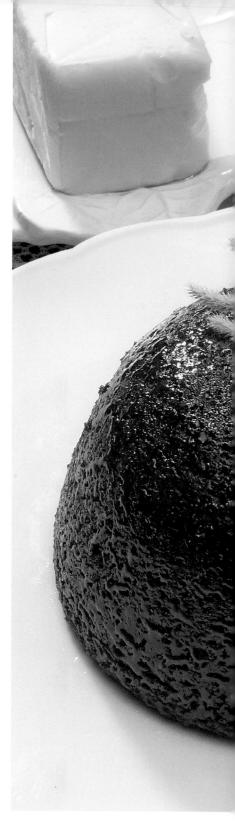

2 Cover with a double thickness of greaseproof paper, making a pleat in the middle. Tie tightly with string, looping it across the centre to make a handle with which to lift the cooked pudding from the pot. Steam for about 3 hours. Serve hot, cut into wedges.

Make the custard by beating the egg yolks and sugar together until light and thick. In a saucepan bring the milk or cream and vanilla close to boiling point but do not allow to boil. Cool slightly and then pour over the eggs and stir until well mixed. Whisk the whiskey (to taste) into the custard. Cook slowly over a very gentle heat until the mixture coats the back of a spoon. Serve the slices of pudding with the custard.

Serves: 4-6
Preparation time: 20'
Cooking time: 3 hr
Difficulty: ●
Flavour: ●●
Kcal (per serving): 906
Proteins (per serving): 19
Fats (per serving): 32
Nutritional Value: ●●●

A poster for Guinness,
Ireland's most famous product.

This pudding is eaten in the Lower Ards area of Ulster at Hallowe'en but also makes a lighter alternative to the traditional Christmas pudding. "Favours", which always include a ring (often just a brass curtain ring), are placed in the pudding at Hallowe'en (for safety wrap these in greaseproof paper).

Whole Poached Salmon

Serves: 10-20 depending on weight of fish
Preparation: 5′
Cooking: 20-40′ depending on weight of fish
Difficulty: ●
Flavour: ●●
Kcal (per serving): 342
Proteins (per serving): 55
Fats (per serving): 13
Nutritional Value: ●●

- 1 whole salmon, gutted
- water/vegetable stock
- dry white wine (optional)

An all-purpose festive dish that is almost mandatory on an Irish buffet table, this is usually served very decoratively, with its skin and scales replaced by very thinly-sliced cucumber.

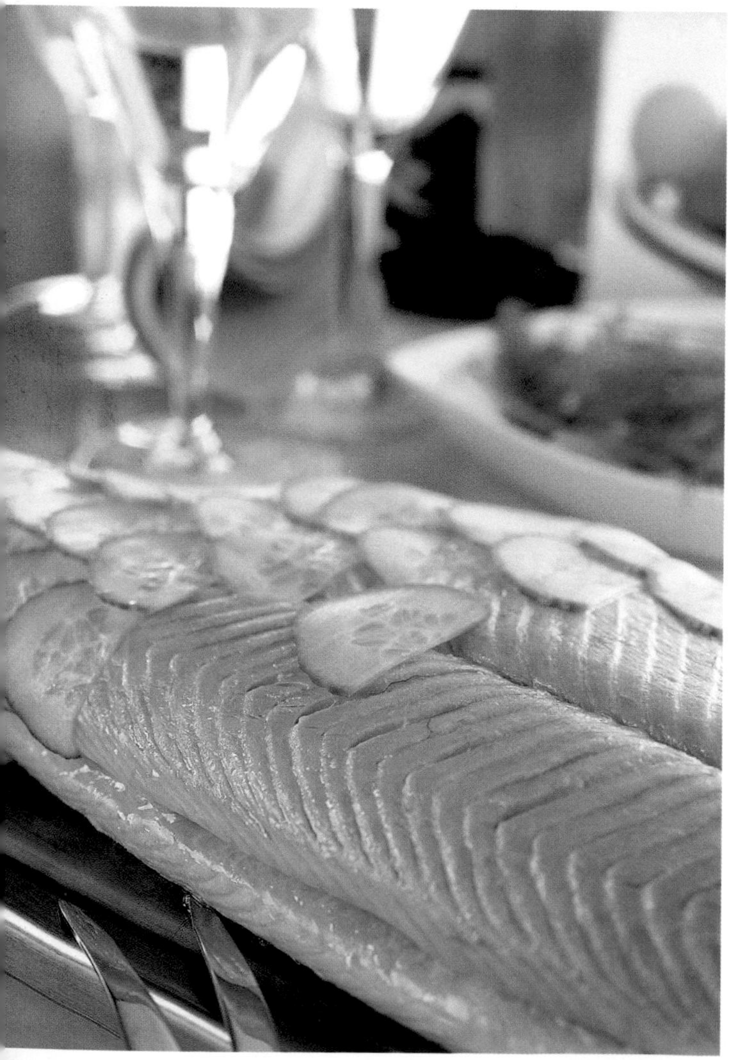

Lay the fish on its side in a fish kettle (on a strip of foil or muslin to enable you to lift it out easily). Pour over just enough water or vegetable stock (add a little dry white wine, if you like) to barely cover. Over a low heat bring it slowly to a bare simmer. Then, if the fish is to be eaten cold, turn off the heat and let the fish cool in the liquid before lifting it out. Before it is completely cold, skin it by slitting the skin along the back and peeling it away.

If the fish is to be eaten hot, continue simmering for 10 minutes for the first 1 kg/2 ¼ lb, or 15 minutes for the second, and 20 minutes for the third. The flesh should be just opaque at the bone and you should be able to easily push a thin skewer into the thickest part of the fish.

Other traditional festive dishes that feature elsewhere in this book are:

for St Brigid's Day
(1 February, the first day of Spring):
Kerry Apple cake page 37
Cider cake page 38
for St Valentines Day *(14 February)*:
Oysters page 47
for Shrove Tuesday:
Pancakes page 14
for St Patrick's Day *(17 March)*:
Corned beef page 57
for Easter:
Lamb with a herb crust page 61
for Lughnasa *(The beginning of the harvest)*:
Fraughan fool page 75
for Hallow'een *(31 October)*:
Barm brack page 34
Colcannon page 22
Boxty page 19
Apple Fadge page 36

Whiskey-tasting at Bushmills Distillery, County Antrim.

Drinks

The Irish climate is unsuitable for growing vines on any scale but wines have been imported since Celtic times, and because of historical political suppression and emigration, many of the great names of French wine growing are Irish. Grains and hops, which thrived in the Irish climate, meant that brewing began early, too, and distinctive beers, cider, mead (a honey-based fermented drink) were widely made and ales, porter and stout – the best known – were developed. Distilling came much later. Historians debate when grain whiskey arrived, although in 1403 the Annals of the Four Masters mentions 'uisce beatha' (water of life).

Irish Coffee

- 1 measure (37.5 ml/2 ½ tablesp) Irish whiskey
- 1 measure strong, hot black coffee (enough to come three-quarters up the glass)
- 2 teasp sugar
- 1-2 tablsp fresh double cream, very, very lightly whipped

Serves: 1

1 Pour the coffee into a warmed wine goblet, add sugar and stir to dissolve. Add whiskey.

2 Position a teaspoon backside up near the rim of the glass and gently pour the cream over the back of the spoon. It should float on the top of the coffee.

You cannot make Irish coffee without sugar because it's the sugar in the mixture that allows the cream to float. The liquid is sipped through the cream, which is never stirred in.

This is probably the best-known Irish whiskey drink. Joe Sheridan, once the chef at the flying-boat base at *Foynes, was definitely its creator despite the fact that Shannon Airport now usually gets the credit.*

Hot Whiskey Punch

- 1 measure (37.5 ml/2 ½ tablesp) Irish whiskey
- 1 slice of lemon
- 3 whole cloves
- boiling water
- sugar (or honey) to taste

W arm a 225 ml/6 fl oz glass by placing a teaspoon in it and pouring in freshly boiled water. The spoon is essential because it absorbs the heat more quickly than the glass and prevents the glass cracking. Working quickly, empty the glass; add the whiskey, lemon, cloves and sweetener. Press the lemon slice to release a little juice. Add boiling water to nearly fill the glass (or whatever amount of water is pleasing to your palate). Stir briefly to dissolve the sweetening and sip while hot.

Also known as a "hot toddy", or a "hot whiskey", this is a great drink to hold and sip on cold, damp winter evenings and is also a popular nightcap. It is the first thing many Irish people think of drinking when they show signs of getting a cold!

Serves: 1

Mudslide

- 1 shot Bailey's Irish Cream liqueur
- 1 shot vodka
- 1 shot crème de cacao
- ice (optional)

Serves: 1

P lace ice, if you are using it, in the bottom of a Martini or medium-sized highball glass. Pour the Bailey's carefully into the glass, followed by the vodka. Drizzle the crème de cacao over a spoon down the inside of the glass to get a 'mudslide' effect.

Irish Flag

- 1 shot crème de menthe
- 1 shot Bailey's Irish Cream liqueur
- 1 shot Hennessy brandy

Serves: 1

1 Pour crème de menthe into the bottom of a glass.

2 Float the Baileys on top, followed by the brandy. The result is a green, white and orange tricolour like the Irish flag.

This colourful and suitably patriotic cocktail is just the thing for raising your glass in a toast to the shamrock on 17 March - St Patrick's Day.

An interior of Bushmills Whiskey Distillery.

Black Velvet

Serves: 4-8 (depending on how much you want to drink)

- 0.75 litre/1 ¼ pint Stout (Guinness, Murphy's, or Beamish), chilled
- 1 bottle of champagne (or prosecco, or cava)

The usual balance between the two liquids is half and half. But it's normal to experiment. So, half-fill a tall glass with stout and add champagne to taste.

This mixture of champagne and stout divides the nation into three groups: those who believe it is a waste of good stout; those who believe it's a waste of champagne; and those who love it as pick-me-up at any time of the day or night.

Sloe Gin

- 0.75 litre bottle of Cork Dry Gin
- 8 peeled almond kernels, or a teaspoon of very high quality almond essence
- 250 g/½ lb sloes (picked after the first frosts)
- 2 tablesp sugar

Makes: 1 litre

Use a sharp fork or a darning needle to prick each berry and then drop it directly into a 1 litre wine bottle. Add the almond kernels, or the almond essence, and the sugar. Fill the bottle with the gin. Cork tightly. Store in a dark place that is not too cold. Shake the bottle once a week for three months. Then allow it to mature undisturbed for a further six months. After that time, strain the liqueur though clean muslin into another bottle and store in a dark place. It will keep for one year. A traditional and much loved country liqueur that may be drunk on its own or used in cocktails.

The Irish Pub

A convivial drink is an essential part of Irish hospitality and a few hours spent in good company in an Irish pub is an experience no visitor should miss. But pubs are much more than just a place to have a drink; they are a gathering place where people find a welcome, congenial company, conversation, warmth, comfort and "a good pint" (usually of stout like Guinness, Beamish or Murphy's), carefully served by experienced barmen and women. Irish people tend to drink spirits in moderation, usually as a "starter" before, or as a "chaser" after, a few pints, and these would usually be their Irish whiskey of preference or Cork Dry Gin.

Early in the day, a traditional pub is a quiet place to read a newspaper and exchange views on what's happening in the world; a place to study racing form (horses and greyhounds) and exchange tips for likely winners with other regular customers.

Historically, in the cities and larger towns some pubs became meeting places for specific groups like politicians, revolutionaries, lawyers, writers and artists, musicians, and so forth. It remains so today; a particular pub may be known as a great sporting pub, a literary pub, an early morning pub (where dockers and market traders

gather), a late night pub where there is *ceol agus craic* – traditional music and lively fun.

What the Irish value most about pub culture is talking to other people. You don't have to know someone to strike up a conversation in an Irish pub. Take a seat at the bar, order your drink, ask a sensible question, or offer a reasonable opinion, and someone is almost sure to engage you in conversation.

Food is served in most pubs at lunchtime. The food offered varies greatly in quality and cost, from plain sandwiches to homemade soda bread with a good soup and a selection of local Irish farmhouse cheeses of superb quality. Many pubs, particularly in the cities and larger towns, have carveries serving roasted and baked meats and (usually) a simple curry, with a selection of plainly cooked vegetables, salads and rice to go with it. While the food is usually rather plain, it is often of very good value.

Then there are the "gourmet" pubs, often located in popular tourist areas, which serve very fine food, superbly cooked. Many of these are near fishing ports and so most serve the local "catch of the day" which is always worth checking out. At the height of the tourist season it is advisable to book ahead.

The Crown Liquor Saloon in Belfast, the Brazen Head, Dublin's oldest pub, and McDaid's pub in Dublin.

The following is a brief selection of atmospheric Irish Pubs:

VAUGHAN'S ANCHOR INN,
Liscannor, County Clare
Just a couple of miles from the famous Cliffs of Moher, the Vaughan family's renowned traditional bar also serves wonderful food at very fair prices. Although famous for his spendid seafood platter, Denis Vaughan cooks everything to order and demands patience from customers for this reason; he can serve up to twenty, often imaginative, fish dishes with locally caught fish. But there are also splendid vegetarian options and superb locally grown beef and lamb as well. They don't take table bookings, so get there early!

THE BRAZEN HEAD,
20 Lr Bridge Street, Dublin 8
Dublin's (possibly Ireland's) oldest pub where drink has been served since the 12th century. The present building is a coaching inn erected about 1700. It is full of character, with lots of nooks and crannies where the chiefs of the United Irishmen used to meet prior to the 1798 Rebellion, and where notable rebels like Robert Emmet, Wolfe Tone and Daniel O'Connell stayed. The pub now serves wholesome food at reasonable prices, and hosts very popular traditional music and jazz nights in the music lounge. A must visit.

THE PORTERHOUSE,
Parliament Street, Temple Bar, Dublin 2
The Porterhouse was Dublin's first micro brewery pub. Ten different beers are brewed on the premises, and a tasting tray is offered. But you don't have to be a beer connoisseur to love this pub. The décor and design is a constant source of delight and the food is a cut above ordinary bar food. This is a real Irish pub in a modern idiom.

THE CROWN LIQUOR SALOON,
46 Great Victoria Street, Belfast
Established in 1826 and later embellished by skilled Italian craftsmen, this is certainly Belfast's most famous pub, an incredibly ornate Victorian gin palace of a type which once thrived in most of Britain's industrial cities. In the centre of the city, the Crown is superbly maintained by The National Trust and, when in Belfast, is a must visit. Eat oysters served on crushed ice, or a bowl of Irish stew in one of its famous "snugs", or visit the restaurant section upstairs which was built with timbers from the sister ship of the Titanic.

INDEX